Why Study Personality?

The Self That Didn't Choose Itself

John Harper

First Edition: December 2025

ISBN: 979-8-9924438-6-8 (Paperback)

HarpGnosis Books

This book is
written for and
dedicated to
YOU
not the patterning
not the history
not the "Hi, I'm…"
but
YOU,
that which is

"Man is a three-brained being. Only when these three brains work in harmony does real understanding appear." — G. I. Gurdjieff

Contents

Foreword

Why Study Personality?

At first glance, the question seems self-evident. Personality offers explanation. It gives language to difference, coherence to behavior, and a sense of orientation in the complexity of human life. In recent years, the Enneagram of Personality has become one of the most widely used frameworks for this purpose, often presented as a way to understand why we think, feel, and act as we do.

And yet, a deeper question remains: *What is personality actually for?*

In *Why Study Personality?*, John Harper reclaims the Enneagram from the increasingly popular tendency to use it as a system of identification. This is not a book about defining oneself more accurately or becoming a more effective version of a familiar identity. It's a book about personality as a functional, adaptive structure—and then, it presents methods to see through it.

From John's perspective, the nine Enneagram personalities are not definers of who we are, but recognizable ways a human ego organizes itself in response to life. Each 'type' represents a patterned strategy of perception, cognition, and emotional regulation *(or not)* that serves an adaptive, formulaic purpose. These structures arise and establish early—shaped by temperament, environment, and necessity. Over time, they solidify into what feels like "my self." What was once fluid becomes fixed. What was once responsive becomes habitual.

My own engagement with the Enneagram has unfolded over two decades of teaching and coaching within relational and developmental contexts. From working with the incarcerated and those severely traumatized to becoming passionate about prevention with a focus on conscious parenting, I've consistently found myself in spaces shaped by the immense realities of the human condition and its impact on human lives.

Along the way, it became clear how early strategies of survival harden into identities we rarely question. I recognize in John Harper a shared passion and conviction that the study of personality must ultimately serve liberation—not just refinement—and that its highest purpose is the easing of the inner contractions. Those that defend against self, others, and reality, deny and prevent the preciousness of self-intimacy, and keep us distanced so greatly from essence, presence, and love itself.

Why Study Personality? is written from this deeper premise. This is not a book about improving one's existing traits, using 'personality' to accept ourselves more, or becoming a more effective version of 'a type'. It's a book about understanding the structure of the ego as it forms 'a sense of self' via an adaptive structure of mind—and then gently, precisely, transcending its confinement.

In this work, the nine Enneagram personality patterns are not presented as descriptions of who we are, but as recognizable ways consciousness organizes itself around experience—in an environment that demands much of us—and a need to survive 'as a self' that's paramount. What begins as essence self-organizes into adaptation and ingrains through repetition. What once protected us begins to limit our contact with our own innocence, beingness, and unabashed spontaneity. How we interpret becomes filtered. How we love becomes conditional. What we seek begins to narrow.

One of John's essential contributions is his insistence that personality is not meant to be perfected, but consciously interrupted, not through force or rejection, but through awareness. The book reveals how our lived reality is continuously shaped by a stream of mental interpretations that quietly stand in for reality itself. Impression by impression, thought by thought, conclusion by conclusion, the mind constructs a world and then reacts to its own conditioned rendering of it.

Again and again, *Why Study Personality?* returns us to what precedes personality altogether. Beneath the patterned meanderings of ego lies a more fundamental *essence*—unstructured, immediate, and luminous. When we lose contact with the grounding of essence though—the motherboard *of sorts* within, identity (and the defense of it) hardens, and suffering follows.

This is where the study of personality becomes a contemplative path. To really see the pattern— with both a reverence and playfulness—is to loosen its grip. To loosen the grip is to rediscover being. And being, when no longer obscured by habituated interpretation, reveals a natural capacity that flows, imbued with receptivity, self- and other-intimacy, and love.

This book does not offer platitudes, nor does it promise transcendence through mere study. Instead, it invites a turning—a gentle reorientation from identification to presence, from mental certainty to lived inquiry, curiosity, exploration, and direct experiencing. Expectation gives way to gratitude. Defense yields to curiosity. And the 'fixed self' relaxes back into the mystery from which its presence initially arose.

A distinguishing feature of John's paradigm-shifting work is his creative application of several systemic mental models for each Enneagram pattern to interrupt *how* personality of a given type perpetuates itself. These models challenge so cleverly where attention narrows, how perception organizes, how habitual conclusions arise, and then defend themselves. By introducing these on-automatic mental inroads with new thinking paradigms, the book restores agency where there was once compulsion, and curiosity where there was once regimented familiarity.

From this foundation, John offers distinct developmental frameworks for each of the nine Enneagram type patterns—not as portraits to identify with, but as lenses through which the patterned mind can be recognized in motion. Each framework is designed to intervene at the level of process rather than content, inviting a loosening of habitual cognition and a softening of the reflex to conclude in a predictable, type-predictable way.

The book is equally grounded in practice. Included are incisive exercises for practitioners—ways of working that support clients in recognizing and stepping out of their default-mode processes. These practices do not aim to prop up the personality from within, but to create the conditions in which awareness can stand apart from it. In that standing apart, something subtle yet profound occurs: the scaffolding of personality structure relaxes, and something essential fills in.

What fills in through relaxation, purports John, is not absence, but presence.

With immense gratitude for what I found in the mind of John's luminous approach, I invite you to this exploration—it's anything but basic or rudimentary. Allow this work to open your mind and heart with a deep compassion for the human condition and a great hope for—and belief in—what lies beyond.

—Suzanne Dion
Certified Enneagram of Personality Teacher and Coach
Co-author with David Daniels, M.D. *"The Enneagram, Relationships, and Intimacy"*
Co-founder, The Attuned Parent Project (TAPP)

Prologue

The Three Doors of Knowing

Where the Prelude spoke of unity as a living experience, this Prologue turns to its architecture—how consciousness expresses through three doors of knowing.

Most people think with their heads, feel with their hearts, and move with their bodies. That is how we describe ourselves—three separate functions, loosely connected, each serving a different purpose. Yet this division is the great misunderstanding of our time. We are not three separate systems; we are a single consciousness expressing itself through three portals of perception.

In the ancient traditions that shaped the Enneagram and informed its later evolution, these three centers—the head, the heart, and the body—were never meant to be hierarchies. They were instruments of attunement, each opening onto a different dimension of reality. The head perceived truth; the heart perceived meaning; the body perceived being. Together they formed one seamless intelligence—knowing, feeling, and acting as one movement of awareness.

Over time, the balance was lost. Civilization grew louder and more complex. We began to mistake mental activity for intelligence, speed for depth, and information for wisdom. The head center, designed to perceive directly, was conscripted into a different task: managing everything. Thought became our governor, our interpreter, our defense. The mind no longer reflected reality; it manufactured it.

We entered the long age of the body-mind split.

It is no accident that so many people today identify as head types. Modern life requires continuous analysis, vigilance, and planning. The mind has become our default operating system. Even those with deeply emotional or instinctual temperaments are trained to interpret their lives through ideas and explanations. The heart feels, but the head narrates. The body knows, but the head vetoes.

The result is a world filled with intelligent people who rarely experience direct knowing. We think about life instead of living it. We understand our feelings rather than just feeling them. We analyze our choices instead of inhabiting them. The head, meant to be an instrument of perception, has become an echo chamber of commentary.

This book does not reject the head—it restores it. It invites the reader to rediscover the head center's true function: illumination. When the mind is quiet enough to perceive rather than process, it becomes a clear mirror of reality. Its gift is not thinking, but seeing.

To study personality, then, is not merely to study ourselves; it is to study the architecture of perception—to see how each Enneagram type expresses a particular distortion in one or more of the centers, and how these distortions obscure our natural clarity.

The head center perceives through clarity and insight. Its intelligence is discriminating, spacious, and precise. When lost, it becomes anxious, abstracted, spinning in its projections. When awake, it perceives directly, without interference, like a still lake reflecting the sky.

The heart center perceives through resonance. It feels the texture of experience—the invisible fabric of relationship, meaning, and belonging. When lost, it clings to emotion and self-image; when awake, it knows unity through compassion, acceptance, and appreciation. Its language is intimacy, not sentimentality.

The body center perceives through immediacy. It is the felt sense of being here—embodied, grounded, responsive. When lost, it becomes willful or inert; when awake, it acts without hesitation, knowing through "Being' doing. Its wisdom is presence in motion.

These three centers are not different kinds of intelligence; they are three facets of one awareness. In a balanced human being, they move together like breath: sensing, feeling, understanding, and acting as one seamless gesture of Being.

In our time, this harmony is rare. We live almost entirely in the head, rarely in the heart, and only accidentally in the body. The head dominates through analysis and control. The heart becomes reactive, overwhelmed by unprocessed feelings. The body becomes mechanical, functioning without consciousness.

This imbalance has not only shaped individuals but also entire civilizations. Our technologies, economies, and even our spiritualities bear the mark of the disembodied mind. We prize the measurable over the meaningful, the conceptual over the experiential, and the efficient over the real.

To live primarily in the head is to inhabit a simulation of life. Thought loops replace direct encounter. Words replace silence. We become narrators of experience instead of participants in it. Yet the head was never meant to lead alone. It was designed to serve the whole. When the head, heart, and body work together, perception becomes multidimensional. The head sees, the heart feels, the body acts—and truth becomes not an idea but an experience.

This book begins where most of us live—in the mind. It speaks to the head not to reinforce its dominance, but to invite its surrender. The Enneagram is used here not as a map of personality but as a mirror of consciousness, showing how the mind organizes experience and how each type of organization filters reality.

Every framework, model, and lens in the chapters that follow has a hidden purpose: to open the head center into direct perception. By tracing how we think, we learn to see the space between thoughts. By watching our interpretations form, we glimpse the silence that precedes them. Gradually, awareness shifts from the activity of the mind to the presence that perceives it.

When the head center opens in this way, it becomes luminous rather than busy. It no longer divides reality; it reveals it. It no longer defends identity; it perceives Being. The intellect, humbled and clarified, becomes a servant of truth.

Yet the restoration of the head alone is not the goal. When perception opens in one center, it naturally resonates through the others. The heart begins to feel without distortion. The body begins to act without conflict. What was fragmented becomes whole again.

Each type in the Enneagram shows how the centers become entangled—how feeling becomes performance, action becomes avoidance, and thought becomes control. But each also reveals the path of return: the movement from compulsion to consciousness, from separation to participation.

The work is not about developing the centers but unblocking them—removing the distortions that prevent their natural functioning. The centers are not built through effort; they are rediscovered through presence.

The rebalancing of the centers is not a spiritual achievement. It is the natural consequence of awareness returning to itself. When the head ceases to dominate, the heart and body remember their intelligence. Feeling deepens, action becomes effortless, and thought turns transparent. Life reclaims its rhythm.

You will recognize this shift when thinking no longer feels heavy. The mind becomes quiet but alert, clear but humble. The heart opens without effort. The body feels alive, awake, responsive. This is not transcendence—it is homecoming.

The journey through this book mirrors that process. It begins in thought, moves through reflection, and ends in direct experience. It is a descent from concept to consciousness.

The Enneagram, at its deepest level, is not a typology but a teaching on how consciousness becomes particular. It shows how Being fractures into patterns of perception and how those patterns can be recognized and released.

In this sense, studying personality is not an intellectual pursuit—it is a sacred act of remembering. To explore your type is to trace the path your awareness took when it became identified with form. It is to find your way back to the place before the split—the place where knowing, feeling, and being were never separate.

This book invites you to turn the head back toward its source, to feel the world through the heart without defense, and to inhabit the body as the living expression of consciousness. It is not a call to think less, but to see more.

When the three centers awaken together, perception no longer divides what it beholds—it becomes the seeing itself. Life reveals itself as wholeness. The head sees the truth, the heart feels its beauty, and the body lives it. This is the human instrument tuned to reality—the harmony we once knew and can know again.

Introduction

The Architecture of Seeing

The Enneagram has been called many things: a personality map, a spiritual system, a diagnostic tool. Yet, at its essence, it is none of these. It is a mirror—a way of seeing how consciousness organizes itself when it falls into identification. It does not describe what we are; it reveals how we lose touch with what we are.

This book, then, is not a manual of types but a study of perception. It examines the ways awareness structures itself, how identity forms, and how personality becomes the organizing field of human experience. Through these structures, the self appears to have continuity, stability, and meaning. But beneath them lies something more fluid and more alive: the movement of Being itself.

To explore personality is to examine the mechanics of this movement—to watch how thought, emotion, and sensation knit themselves into a self. When observed closely, the pattern begins to loosen. Awareness ceases to be trapped inside it and begins to perceive itself as the ground of all experience.

The book unfolds through multiple lenses—psychological, philosophical, and phenomenological—each one opening a different way of seeing. These lenses are not competing viewpoints but complementary perspectives that allow the reader to observe from many angles at once. As in the facets of a diamond, each reflection reveals more of the whole.

The Framework of the Book

Why Study Personality? is divided into five parts, each corresponding to a distinct movement of inquiry.

> **Part One**, *The Question*, asks why we study personality at all. It introduces the paradox that drives the human search: our desire for self-knowledge and our simultaneous resistance to it.

> **Part Two**, *The Human Mechanism*, explores how personality forms—the architecture of perception, the loss of Being, and the mechanism of resistance. Here, the Enneagram is introduced as a mirror rather than a map, revealing the automatic patterns that sustain ego identity.

Part Three, *The Nine Mirrors*, examines each of the nine types as a distinct way in which consciousness distorts reality. Each type is both a defense and a reflection of essence lost. To study one's type is to explore the shape of one's forgetting.

Part Four, *The Path Beyond Type*, moves from structure to movement—from the mechanics of personality to the possibility of transformation. It is not about transcending type but about discovering what is untouched by it.

Part Five, *The Mirror Self Series*, applies these insights directly. Each type is explored through a triad of lenses—a mental model, a system of thinking, and a framework for practice. These lenses are not to be adopted as doctrines but as instruments of awareness. They are meant to open perception, not to define it.

How to Engage with this Book

This book is not written to be scanned. It is a contemplative text, an experiment in awareness disguised as a study of personality. Its purpose is not to inform the mind but to awaken it.

You will notice that each part of the book alternates between conceptual exposition and experiential reflection. This rhythm is intentional. The conceptual material engages the head center—the part of us that seeks clarity and understanding. The reflective passages and exercises engage the heart and body centers, grounding understanding in lived presence.

The movement between these modes mirrors the journey the book describes: from knowing to seeing, from thinking to being. The goal is not to accumulate insight but to witness how insight arises and fades, how meaning reorganizes itself when attention becomes quiet.

Each chapter, particularly in Part Five, is designed as a lens—an invitation to perception rather than a conclusion. You are not being asked to agree or disagree, but to look through. What matters is not what the text says but what begins to stir in you as you read.

The frameworks and models presented are not final truths, but mirrors for inquiry. Each invites the reader to watch their mind in motion—to see how thought interprets, resists, and reframes experience. The real study is not of personality as a concept but of personality as a phenomenon, alive in real time.

A Way of Reading

To read this book well, read slowly. Allow each paragraph to land before you move to the next. Pause when something resonates, confuses, or unsettles. These are thresholds—moments when your habitual ways of knowing are being gently stretched.

As you progress, notice not only what you think but what you experience. How does your attention behave as you read? Do you drift, tighten, analyze, or resist? Each reaction is part of the study. The reader's experience is the living laboratory of this work.

If you are a student of the Enneagram, this book will deepen your understanding by showing how the types are not fixed patterns but living processes. If you are a teacher or practitioner, it will offer language and frameworks for guiding others into direct contact with experience. But above all, this book is for the curious— curious about how awareness turns into identity, and how identity can dissolve back into awareness.

You may find that the book's meaning changes as you return to it. That, too, is intentional. The text is alive; it evolves with the reader. What seems obscure in one reading may open like a flower in another. The understanding is not cumulative but emergent.

This is not a linear journey of self-improvement. It is an inward turning—a study of how perception organizes, contracts, and reopens. Every concept points back to a single realization: that **awareness is the true subject of all inquiry.**

As you move through these pages, remember that nothing here is final. Every framework, every model, every reflection is a doorway; step through, then look back. The one who looks—the one who sees—is what this book is really about.

Lens of Perception

Mental Model + Thinking System + Framework = Lens of Perception

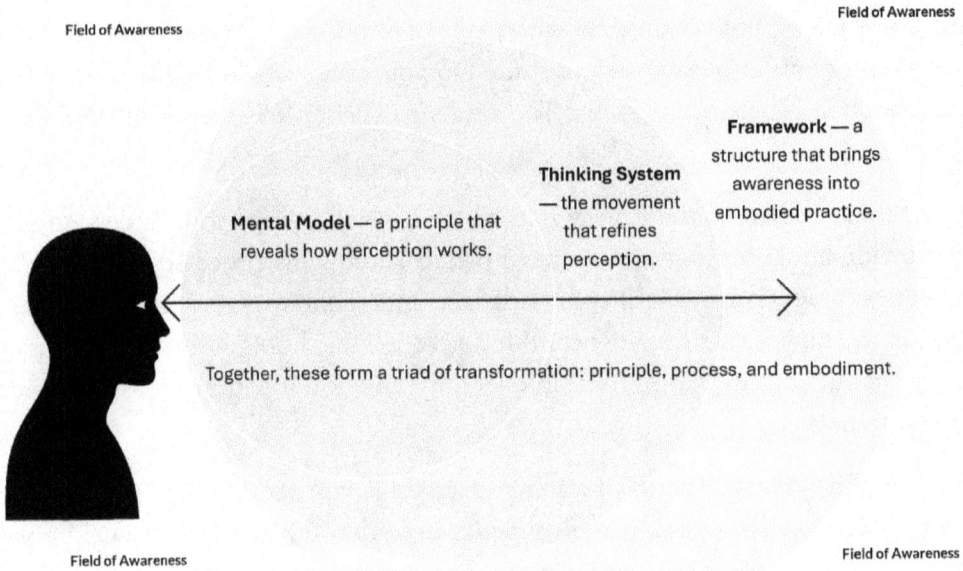

Field of Awareness

Field of Awareness

Framework — a structure that brings awareness into embodied practice.

Thinking System — the movement that refines perception.

Mental Model — a principle that reveals how perception works.

Together, these form a triad of transformation: principle, process, and embodiment.

Field of Awareness

Field of Awareness

Part One

The Question

(Inversion + Fractal Thinking, through Appreciative Inquiry)

Why Explore Personality

Most people study personality to improve it, aiming to become happier, more successful, more lovable, and more efficient. But what if we turn the question around? What if personality is not something to be polished, but something to be seen through?

Inversion turns the familiar lens around. Instead of asking how to improve our personality, we ask what our personality type conceals or compensates for. Instead of fixing the surface, we turn toward what it hides or tries to mimic. Personality is not the mask we must perfect; it is the echo of a long-forgotten song.

Fractal Thinking helps us see how each small reflection of our personality—every preference, defense, and compulsion—is a repeating pattern of the larger shape of our adaptation. Just as a coastline repeats its jagged edge in miniature, the personality repeats its loss of Being in countless ways.

Through **Appreciative Inquiry**, we do not condemn these patterns; instead, we marvel at their ingenuity. Each Enneagram fixation is love's attempt to remain connected. Each distortion carries a seed of the essence it once reflected. The beginning, then, is not to polish the surface but to see how even the cracks point back to the sea beneath.

The Trend Today

Personality studies today are marketed as ways to succeed: know your type, amplify your strengths, avoid your weaknesses. This approach seems useful—but Inversion asks us to question whether success is the point at all.

If personality is the trance, then perfecting it deepens the trance. We may optimize our habits, but optimization is not the same as awakening. The fixation becomes shinier, more marketable—but it is still fixation.

Fractal Thinking reveals the trap: **the same drive that seeks to improve is the pattern repeating**. The Enneagram Type Three's desire to become more valuable is the fractal echo of the very loss of value it conceals. The Six's craving for certainty repeats endlessly, but certainty never arrives. Each personality type repeats its strategy like a fractal spiral, turning back into itself, tighter and tighter.

Inquiry softens this inversion. Rather than dismissing modern personality work, we recognize its underlying gift: people long to know themselves. The hunger for self-knowledge, however misdirected, is sacred. By acknowledging this longing, we can redirect it: away from polishing the surface, toward seeing how the surface hides the depth.

Origins and Purpose of the Enneagram

The Enneagram did not begin as a personality typing system. Its origins point to the process of transformation, the Law of Three, and the Law of Seven—the fractal architecture of existence. It mapped how Being descends into form and how form returns to Being.

Through the lens of Inversion, we reinterpret its purpose. Instead of asking which type we are, we ask where we are stuck in the process of remembering. The Enneagram is not about categories but about interruptions. It shows the shock points—the moments where the soul's flow was diverted into survival rather than presence.

Fractal Thinking reveals the Enneagram as a recursive map. The nine types are not boxes but repeating patterns of loss. Each point reflects the whole, just as a single spiral of a nautilus shell contains the curve of the entire form.

The Enneagram is not a typology but a fractal geometry of forgetting and remembering.

Appreciative Inquiry integrates this insight. Each type is not only a wound but also a doorway.

- The Ennea-Type Three's deceit hides a seed of radiant value.
- The Five's avarice protects the possibility of true knowing.
- The Eight's intensity shields a deeper innocence.

Appreciating the hidden gift in each type reveals that even our distortions are expressions of love trying to return home.

The Enneagram's true purpose, then, is not to define us but to remind us that we are not our patterns, but the Being that shines through them.

Personality and the Loss of Being

Personality begins as adaptation: a strategy to secure love, belonging, and survival in a world estranged from Being. Here again, Inversion helps: what we think of as 'self' is actually the opposite of self. It is the shape of absence, the memory of what was lost.

Fractal Thinking shows this clearly. Each personality type is not unique in its essence, but rather a variation of the same recursive event: essence disrupted, a survival strategy created, and repetition established.

Enneagram Type One's pursuit of perfection, the Two's offering of love, the Nine's merging—all echo the original fracture, repeating the loss of Being in their shape.

This repetition is not only psychological; it is temporal. The child who once learned to perform for love continues this gesture into adolescence, in their work, relationships, and spirituality. The fractal repeats through every decade of life. No matter how sophisticated the outer form, the inner pattern is the same.

From the appreciative lens, we honor these strategies. The child did not fail by becoming a personality; the child succeeded in staying alive. The cocoon of type is not a mistake but a shelter, woven until the soul could find its way back. To appreciate the cocoon is to recognize it as the necessary architecture through which the butterfly of presence emerges.

Loss of Being is not the end. It is the beginning of the journey back to what was never truly gone.

Resistance: Ego's Gravity

Every lost soul (identified with the ego) longs for freedom and simultaneously resists it through ego identification. Here, Inversion asks us: **What if resistance is not the obstacle but the way?**

Fractal Thinking reveals how resistance repeats itself at every level. It is not a single wall but a pattern: physical tension, emotional defense, intellectual avoidance. Each instance is a miniature of the whole gravitational pull of the ego identity.

This orbit is self-similar across scales. A small withdrawal in a conversation mirrors a lifetime of retreat. A single tightening in the chest mirrors the universal fear of dissolution. Each expression of resistance is the whole repeating itself.

Appreciative Inquiry transforms resistance from enemy to teacher. Every contraction shows us where we are protecting something tender. Every avoidance signals a fear of dissolution. Instead of fighting resistance, we can appreciate it as love's way of saying, "Not yet." When held gently, resistance reveals the wound it guards—and beyond the wound, the essence it protects.

Resistance is not an enemy but a disguised presence. To meet it with curiosity is to turn gravity into flight.

The Turning Point of Attention

Every contraction longs to open. Every pattern of resistance carries within it the memory of freedom. The shift from resistance to flow begins not through effort, but through attention.

*When attention turns from what we resist to
how we resist, something fundamental changes.*

In that moment, consciousness begins to see itself. The tightening that once felt like protection is revealed as fear of dissolution. The avoidance that once seemed self-preserving is seen as a barrier to what is longed for.

Attention becomes alchemical: what it touches begins to soften.

This turning point is not about fixing or transcending the ego. It is about *seeing* it.

*The ego cannot free itself by will; it can only
become transparent when awareness is brought*

4

directly to the pattern, without judgment or strategy.

What was once a defensive posture becomes a doorway.

Inversion reveals that personality is not a self to be perfected but an adaptive survival mechanism shaped by loss and longing.

Fractal Thinking shows how every gesture of our type is a miniature of the entire journey of forgetting and remembering—each moment of attention rippling through the whole field of our being, loosening what once felt fixed.

Through Appreciative Inquiry, we learn to honor these patterns rather than condemn them, recognizing that each adaptation is love in disguise, and that every turning of attention inward becomes a threshold of transparency.

Resistance, rather than an obstacle, becomes a guide. Its pull reveals precisely where life wants to flow again.

The shift is subtle yet irreversible: **attention ceases to orbit the problem and begins to illuminate it.**

> What was gravity becomes guidance.
> What was tension becomes tenderness.

And in this simple reorientation, the possibility of freedom appears—not as escape, but as intimacy with what is.

Part One invites us not to improve the self, but to ask the deeper question:

Who is the one trying to improve?

5

Part Two

The Human Mechanism

(Law of Reversed Effort + Temporal Thinking, through Appreciative Inquiry)

Why study personality?
By understanding how awareness becomes
divided, we rediscover the seamless intelligence
that was never divided in the first place.

Personality and the Loss of Being

Again, personality begins as adaptation. The infant enters a world radiant and undefended, but the world it meets is not ready for such openness. Love may be present, but it is not unconditional. Presence may be offered, but it is interrupted. What is natural soon learns to bend.

Here, the **Law of Reversed Effort** makes itself known. The more the child strains to secure a sense of belonging, the more precarious that belonging becomes— because effort introduces self-consciousness, and self-consciousness fractures the natural flow of connection. The more the child learns to please, the more approval feels like survival—and the less spontaneous love can be trusted. Every strategy of effort deepens the sense of deficiency it was meant to resolve.

Over time, this struggle accumulates. **Temporal Thinking** shows us how adaptation layers itself across the decades. The first smiles designed to win affection repeat in adolescence as a performance for peers, reappear in adulthood as a compulsion to achieve, and reappear in spiritual life as the need to be seen as good, awakened, and worthy. The fractal of effort spans the entire arc of life. What was once a small shift in childhood becomes a lifelong orbit.

Personality is not an invention but a sediment. It solidifies from countless repetitions of effort, each one attempting to restore contact with Being but only burying it further. The more effort, the greater the distance.

6

Appreciative Inquiry reminds us to bow to this ingenuity. The child, in its helplessness, crafted strategies that worked. The personality is not a flaw but a testimony to survival. It held the soul together through a world that could not mirror it. The cocoon of self was love's creation. To see it this way is to recognize that even loss carries devotion within it.

Loss of Being, then, is not an error to be blamed but a condition to be understood. It is the beginning of the path home.

Yielding to the Pull

Resistance does not vanish through effort; it reveals its intelligence through surrender. What we call resistance is not a single obstruction but a living tension—the meeting place between what is ready to be born and what is still afraid to die. Every contraction holds both forces at once: the instinct to preserve and the invitation to dissolve.

When we push against resistance, we strengthen its orbit. But when we allow its pull to be felt without opposition, something subtle begins to shift. Awareness enters the field of resistance like light entering water. The density does not disappear; it becomes transparent. The very movement that once bound us now guides us toward depth.

Yielding does not mean resignation. It means ceasing to insist that life unfold differently than it does. The energy once spent in control returns as presence. In the moment we stop trying to escape resistance, we begin to experience its interior shape—the longing, the fear, the tenderness it protects.

Resistance, held in awareness,
becomes revelation.

Temporal Thinking reminds us that yielding is rarely sudden. The same patterns that repeat across a lifetime also loosen gradually. A softening in the body precedes an opening in the heart; a glimpse of compassion ripples backward through years of defense. Change does not occur by replacing resistance with acceptance, but by entering the very texture of resistance until its edges dissolve.

Appreciative Inquiry teaches us to bow to this process. Each hesitation, each tightening, each "not yet" is an act of care—life's way of pacing revelation so it does not overwhelm. To yield to resistance is to trust its timing.

In that trust, the ego's gravity relaxes. What once pulled inward now expands outward, as though the orbit itself were remembering the sun around which it turns.

Acceptance and the Return to Flow

If resistance is the soul's contraction through identification with the self-image, acceptance is the release. Yet here again, the Law of Reversed Effort reveals a paradox: **the harder we try to accept, the less acceptance is possible**. Effort turns acceptance into another strategy of control. True acceptance arises only when effort ceases.

Temporal Thinking demonstrates how acceptance expands over time. At first, it may appear as a fleeting glimpse—a moment where we stop rejecting and allow reality to be as it is. Over months and years, these moments accumulate, slowly reshaping the ground of identification into transparency. Acceptance begins as a crack in the dam and becomes, with time, the return of the entire river to its course.

Acceptance is not resignation. It is intimacy with experience. To stop dividing life into wanted and unwanted is to allow Being to flow again without obstruction. A single act of inclusion ripples across the whole field of the soul, just as a single moment of rejection once created a lifetime of contraction.

Appreciative Inquiry reframes acceptance as gratitude. What once felt like an enemy is recognized as a messenger. Fear reveals courage. Shame discloses the longing for innocence. Anger uncovers serenity. Every emotion, when allowed, shows its hidden essence. Acceptance is the recognition that even the most painful experiences hold wisdom.

To accept is to return to flow. The personality remains, but it is no longer the center of gravity. It becomes transparent, an instrument rather than a prison. The soul begins to move again in accordance with its natural design.

The Law of Reversed Effort suggests that the harder we strive to change ourselves, the deeper we entrench our existing patterns. Temporal Thinking reveals how these patterns stretch across years, repeating the same story in new forms. Appreciative Inquiry teaches us that even these repetitions are acts of devotion—brilliant adaptations that carried us until we were ready to remember.

Part Two reveals the human mechanism not as an error to be eliminated but as a pattern to be honored, understood, and gently released.

Part Three

The Mirrored Self

(Signal vs. Noise + Empathic Thinking, through Appreciative Inquiry)

The Nine Mirrors

The Enneagram does not reveal who we are in essence. It reveals how we mistake noise for signal. Each Enneagram Type is like a radio tuned slightly off frequency: static fills the air, yet a true transmission hums underneath. The fixation is the noise, the distortion. The signal is the essence that was always there, waiting to be heard.

- **Signal vs. Noise** trains us to discern what is essential from what is interference.
- **Empathic Thinking** allows us to feel into the longing beneath the distortion.
- **Appreciative Inquiry** helps us honor each type as both wound and promise.

Each type can be seen as a mirror. At first, the mirror shows us the noise—our defenses, our compulsions, our strategies. But if we look with empathy, we begin to see what the mirror reflects beneath the distortion: the soul's attempt to preserve contact with Being.

- **Type One – The Search for Rightness**
  - **Noise:** harsh judgment, perfectionism, endless correction. The One hears every note of discord and tightens against it. Effort rises, and the more effort, the more tension.
  - **Signal:** serenity, the natural harmony of Being. The One's longing is for the quiet rightness that needs no improvement.
  - **Empathic view:** the One's anger is not cruelty but grief for the lost sense of inherent order.
  - **Appreciative Inquiry** reminds us that this very striving carries the memory of wholeness. What the One seeks outside is already waiting within.

10

- **Type Two – The Gift and the Hunger for Love**
  - **Noise:** over-giving, intrusion, seduction. The Two pours attention outward, needing to be needed. The more love is chased, the more dependent love becomes.
  - **Signal:** unconditional love, the boundless abundance of Being. The Two's pride hides a tender longing to be loved simply for existing.
  - **Empathic view:** the Two's compulsive giving is not manipulation at its root, but a child's strategy to ensure love would not disappear.
  - **Appreciative Inquiry** reveals the gift here: beneath the noise of helping is the infinite signal of love.

- **Type Three – The Performer and the Loss of Value**
  - **Noise:** image, deceit, achievement. The Three builds a self out of accomplishments, fearing collapse if the mask is dropped.
  - **Signal:** radiant value, the innate recognition of Being's worth. No performance can add to it, and no failure can subtract from it.
  - **Empathic view:** the Three's drive is not greed but survival, born from a moment when value felt conditional.
  - **Appreciative Inquiry** teaches us to see the honesty hidden inside the deceit: the longing simply to rest in the truth of one's being.

- **Type Four – The Romantic and the Longing for Depth**
  - **Noise:** envy, comparison, drama. The Four gazes at what is missing, amplifying the ache of absence.
  - **Signal:** equanimity, the fullness of ordinary life. Wholeness is not elsewhere—it is here, waiting to be included.
  - **Empathic view:** the Four's grief is not self-indulgence but devotion to lost depth.
  - **Appreciative Inquiry** helps us see that within every ache lies the promise of completeness. The longing is love calling to be remembered.

- **Type Five – The Observer and the Retreat from Knowing**
  - **Noise:** withdrawal, withholding, avarice. The Five gathers knowledge yet withholds self, fearing depletion.

- **Signal:** wisdom, spontaneous knowing through presence. True knowing requires no hoarding—it arises from direct intimacy with life.
- **Empathic view:** the Five's avarice is not miserliness but protection of a fragile flame of knowing.
- **Appreciative Inquiry** reframes this withholding as devotion to truth. The Five's retreat hides a gift: the capacity for pure, immediate insight.

- **Type Six – The Loyalist and the Loss of Faith**
  - **Noise:** doubt, anxiety, projection. The Six scans the horizon for danger, endlessly preparing for what may come.
  - **Signal:** faith, the grounded confidence that Being supports life in every moment.
  - **Empathic view:** the Six's fear is not cowardice but love looking for a safe home.
  - **Appreciative Inquiry** allows us to see their vigilance as fidelity to trust itself. Beneath the noise of doubt, the signal of courage is waiting.

- **Type Seven – The Enthusiast and the Flight from Pain**
  - **Noise:** gluttony, distraction, endless stimulation. The Seven leaps from one possibility to another, fleeing the confinement of pain.
  - **Signal:** contentment, the quiet joy of Being. Joy does not depend on novelty but arises from the freedom of presence.
  - **Empathic view:** the Seven's flight is not frivolity but reverence for freedom, born from a time when pain felt overwhelming.
  - **Appreciative Inquiry** helps us see that even in distraction, the Seven carries the memory of joy.

- **Type Eight – The Challenger and the Loss of Innocence**
  - **Noise:** control, domination, intensity. The Eight pushes against life with force, fearing vulnerability as weakness.
  - **Signal:** true strength, the undefended openness of Being. Innocence is not weakness but power in its purest form.
  - **Empathic view:** the Eight's lust for control is not cruelty but protection against betrayal.

- o **Appreciative Inquiry** reveals the tenderness hidden beneath the armor: the longing to trust again in the power of love.

- **Type Nine – The Peacemaker and the Forgetting of Self**
  - o **Noise:** inertia, merging, indolence. The Nine drifts into comfort, diffusing attention into others, forgetting their presence.
  - o **Signal:** awake participation, the unity of Being. The Nine's essence is action arising from the fullness of presence.
  - o **Empathic view:** the Nine's indolence is not laziness but grief for the lost sense of connection.
  - o **Appreciative Inquiry** reframes their merging as devotion to unity. Beneath the noise of forgetting lies the signal of wholeness already intact.

Signal vs. Noise shows us that personality is interference, not identity. Empathic Thinking helps us tune our ear to the longing beneath each distortion. Appreciative Inquiry reminds us that every fixation is not a problem to be fixed, but a doorway into essence.

The Nine Mirrors are not judgments but invitations. Each type reflects both wound and promise, distortion and essence. To study them is to learn how to tune our attention from noise to signal, until the clear voice of Being is heard again.

Part Four

The Path Beyond Type

(Friction Reduction + Principle of Least Effort, through Appreciative Inquiry)

Conscious Suffering and Radical Allowing

Recognition is the first step, but freedom requires more than seeing the pattern. Transformation arises only through direct, sustained contact with what we habitually avoid.

This is conscious suffering—not the punishment of the soul, but the willingness to remain present with discomfort long enough for it to reveal its truth.

Friction Reduction shows why this matters. Most of our suffering does not come from what is happening, but from the friction of resisting it. A difficult feeling, on its own, passes quickly, but resistance clings to it, replaying, explaining, pushing it away. The more we resist, the more heat we generate, until the friction burns us.

The **Principle of Least Effort** points to another way. Effort belongs to the personality, whose nature is striving. Presence arises when striving relaxes. Allowing is not passive but intimate—it lets experience unfold without interference. The river does not need to be pushed; it simply finds its way through and around the rocks that resist it.

Conscious suffering is the practice of relaxing into what arises rather than trying to reshape it.

The contraction becomes transparent not through effort but through inclusion. To feel shame without fleeing into justification, to meet fear without collapsing into control, to sit with longing without rushing to fill it—this is conscious suffering.

Appreciative Inquiry reorients us to see even suffering as carrying intelligence. Fear signals where courage waits. Anger conceals serenity. Emptiness hides fullness. Suffering becomes not an obstacle but a teacher, pointing us toward the qualities of Being that were never lost.

14

Conscious suffering is not grim endurance but luminous intimacy. It is the fire in which personality softens and presence is revealed.

> **Contemplative practice:** Sit quietly and sense your Ennea-Type's familiar pattern. Do not attempt to change it. Instead, ask, "What quality of Being is this pattern protecting?" Allow the answer to arise not in thought but in felt experience. Watch how the fixation softens as its hidden gift begins to shine.

From Personality to Presence

Personality and presence are not opposites, but stages of the same unfolding process. Personality is Being's first attempt to know itself through form, a provisional identity shaped by loss. Presence is that same Being remembering its source.

Friction Reduction reveals the path of transition. The more we push against personality, the tighter it contracts. The more we soften around it, the more transparent it becomes. Struggle adds friction, while receptivity reduces it. Personality loosens not by force but by gentleness.

The Principle of Least Effort explains why striving fails.

Awakening does not dawn through achievement.

Presence arises when effort ceases, when the one who strives to awaken steps aside. The greatest movement is the least effortful: simply resting in what is.

Appreciative Inquiry helps us reinterpret personality. Instead of an enemy to be destroyed, personality becomes an instrument. Its patterns remain, but they no longer define us. Ennea-Type Three may still perform, but the performance becomes expression rather than compulsion. The Five may still reflect, but reflection becomes wisdom rather than withholding. Each type becomes a channel through which essence can play its music.

As presence deepens, what once seemed lost returns naturally. Strength, love, clarity, joy, peace—all reemerge, not as achievements but as the qualities of Being itself. The self that once strove dissolves, and the ego self becomes transparent to its origins.

Being as the Real Self

At the end of the path, there is no path. **What began as inquiry dissolves into immediacy.** The seeker, the search, and the structure all vanish into what has always been here: Being aware of itself.

Friction Reduction is complete. There is no longer resistance, no longer opposition. The Principle of Least Effort reveals itself as truth: life unfolds by itself, without striving, without interference.

Appreciative Inquiry turns our gaze to wonder. Every fixation, every resistance, every adaptation was an expression of Being knowing itself in form. The forgetting was not a failure but part of the remembering. The Enneagram circle closes: descent into manifestation and return to Unity are viewed as a single, continuous movement.

Here, there is only simplicity—the silent joy of existence without agenda. Personality becomes a translucent vessel, and Being shines through as the real self.

And so, the study of personality ends where it began—not with the self we construct, but with the awareness that perceives through it.

> **Closing reflection:** To rediscover presence is to see that nothing was ever missing. The self that didn't choose itself was never the end of the story. Beneath it, the Being that was never lost has been looking through our eyes all along.

Part Five

The Prism of Type

Nine Patterns, One Light

The enneagram shows us nine ways the light of being refracts into personality. Each type is not a cage but a prism, bending awareness into a recognizable pattern—rigid in its habit, predictable in its logic, yet luminous at its core.

In this part, we turn to each of the nine Ennea-Types, not to describe them in detail, but to work with them as living exercises in self-reflection. Each chapter follows the same three movements:

1. **The Human Mechanism** – exploring the automatic habits of type.

2. **The Mirror Self** – seeing the reflection that type throws back.

3. **The Path Beyond Type** – stepping into awareness beyond personality.

To open new perspectives, each type is paired with three unique combinations of mental models and systems of thinking, along with one guiding framework. These are not explanations to memorize but lenses to try on. They are experiments in loosening the grip of type and discovering how flexible, playful, and dynamic awareness can be.

The invitation is simple:

- See your type as a prism, not a prison.
- Notice how each lens shifts what you see.
- Stay with the exercises, not for answers, but for fresh encounters with yourself.

Nine types. Nine prisms. Nine doors leading back to the same light.

Type One

The Search for Rightness

The Human Mechanism

Opening Lens

First Principles Thinking + Critical Thinking, through DMAIC brings together two complementary modes of inquiry inside a disciplined framework.

First Principles Thinking strips a problem to its irreducible truths, bypassing assumptions and conventions.

Critical Thinking adds rigor by testing logic, identifying biases, and evaluating evidence.

The **DMAIC framework (Define, Measure, Analyze, Improve, Control)** then structures this combined lens into an actionable cycle: defining what is actually at issue, measuring data rather than impressions, analyzing patterns without distortion, improving by applying fresh insight, and controlling to sustain change.

Together, this trio trains attention to cut through surface explanations, reach the root of personality habits, and guide reflection into practical transformation.

Why this lens?

Type One habitually polishes the surface of reality, correcting flaws without touching the root.

First Principles Thinking cuts through this surface noise, stripping assumptions down to their most basic truths.

Critical Thinking sharpens this cut, challenging internalized voices of "should" and "must."

Paired with *DMAIC*, a framework EnneaType Ones already run unconsciously, this lens turns their compulsion for improvement into a mirror for inquiry.

Exploration: Every EnneaType One knows the tightening of the body in the presence of disorder. The DMAIC cycle explains the reflex: Define, Measure,

Analyze, Improve, Control. But what if the same framework became an instrument of reflection instead of compulsion?

Exercise:

- **Define:** Recall three moments of irritation. Instead of listing errors, ask: *What principle was I trying to protect?*
- **Measure:** Notice how your body feels when you hold those principles. Where does rightness already exist within you, independent of events?
- **Analyze:** Ask: *Whose standard am I enforcing?* Trace it to parents, teachers, culture—or your own Being.
- **Improve:** Experiment: *What if I honored the principle without correcting anything?*
- **Control:** For one day, loosen control over one small imperfection. Watch what happens. This is not abandoning rightness—it is returning to its root, where serenity waits beneath striving.

The Mirror Self

Opening Lens

Law of Contrast + Root Cause Analysis, through DMAIC uses the power of difference to reveal hidden causes.

The **Law of Contrast** sharpens awareness by setting one experience against another — light against dark, tension against release.

Root Cause Analysis digs beneath symptoms to uncover the deeper forces shaping behavior.

The **DMAIC cycle (Define, Measure, Analyze, Improve, Control)** provides this inquiry structure: define the problem, measure what changes across contexts, analyze the contrast to identify hidden drivers, improve by addressing the real cause, and control by sustaining clarity.

Together, this lens trains perception to see not only what is happening, but why it is happening, and how opposite conditions reveal the foundations of personality patterns.

Why this lens?

Ones view life through contrast: right/wrong, pure/impure. This sharpens discernment but also exaggerates flaws.

The Law of Contrast makes the distortion explicit, showing how judgment depends on comparison.

Root Cause Analysis drills beneath symptoms, exposing the grief beneath perfectionism—the longing for a harmony once lost.

With *DMAIC* as a backdrop, this combination turns Type One's evaluative machinery inward.

Exploration: EnneaType One's mirror exaggerates noise until the signal disappears. But contrast itself is not evil—it points back to a deeper root. Beneath correction lies longing.

Exercise:

- Choose one irritation. Write it down.
- List three opposite qualities you wish were present.
- Now reverse the first three steps of DMAIC by starting at the depth rather than the surface:
    - Analyze: Sense into the grief and longing beneath this irritation. What does this reaction reveal that you most deeply wish were true? Put this into a single sentence that begins with "I long for..."
    - Measure: Look back over the last week and notice how often this same longing has appeared but gone unseen—through criticism, tightening, or correction. Jot down three situations where the longing was present but disguised as fault-finding.
    - Define: Rewrite the original "problem" not as a flaw to be fixed, but as a statement of longing. For example, instead of "People are so sloppy," define it as "I long for a world where care and integrity are honored."

This way, the sequence moves from analyzing longing to measuring its invisibility to redefining the problem from flaw to desire—an actual inversion of the usual DMAIC flow.

As the mirror clears, correction is revealed as love's disguise.

The Path Beyond Type

Opening Lens

The Map is Not the Territory + Scenario Planning, through DMAIC challenges the tendency to mistake mental models for reality.

The Map is Not the Territory reminds us that concepts, labels, and strategies are only representations, never the living terrain itself.

Scenario Planning complements this by opening multiple possible futures, refusing to collapse uncertainty into a single outcome.

The **DMAIC framework (Define, Measure, Analyze, Improve, Control)** grounds this process: define the current map in use, measure its limits, analyze alternative scenarios, improve by expanding perspective, and control by maintaining flexibility rather than clinging to one fixed path.

Together, this lens exposes how our inner maps constrain perception and invites us to plan with openness, adapting to reality as it unfolds rather than forcing reality to fit our ideas.

Why this lens?

Ones cling to maps—mental blueprints of how life should unfold. But maps are never the territory. This is the crack where freedom begins.

The Map is Not the Territory interrupts the illusion that life must match the diagram.

Scenario Planning helps loosen rigidity by imagining multiple futures in which peace remains possible.

Paired with *DMAIC*, this combination retools the perfectionist's cycle into a practice of flexibility.

Exploration: Life resists maps. The world is not wrong—the diagram is incomplete. What if rightness comes not from control, but from openness to possibility?

Exercise:

- Make two columns: "Map" and "Territory." Write three ideals under "Map" (e.g., "I should never make mistakes"). Describe reality under "Territory."

- For each, imagine three scenarios where the "Territory" is imperfect yet peace is still present.
- Use DMAIC inverted:
  - Define possibility, not flaw.
  - Measure your body's response to holding multiple outcomes.
  - Analyze which scenario loosens judgment.
  - Improve by leaning into flexibility.
  - Control by releasing control.

This practice teaches the One that serenity is not achieved by perfecting reality but by meeting it directly.

Closing Invitation for Type One

Type One has been given four lenses:

- First Principles Thinking + Critical Thinking

- Law of Contrast + Root Cause Analysis

- The Map is Not the Territory + Scenario Planning

- All grounded in the DMAIC cycle you already know by heart.

See what happens when you let these lenses rotate your seeing. Each one loosens the rut of correction, expanding your capacity for self-reflection. The invitation is not to become a better type, but to remember that rightness is already here, shining through the cracks.

Type Two

The Gift and Hunger for Love

The Human Mechanism

Opening Lens

Circle of Competence + Reframing, through the GROW Model, encourages reflection on both limits and possibilities.

The **Circle of Competence** asks us to recognize what we truly understand versus where we overreach, clarifying the boundaries of reliable knowledge and skill.

Reframing then shifts the angle of vision, turning obstacles into openings and problems into possibilities.

The **GROW Model (Goal, Reality, Options, Way Forward)** provides direction for this process: define the goal, face the reality within your circle of competence, explore options through reframing, and choose a way forward that honors both strength and growth.

Together, this lens creates a disciplined yet imaginative approach to self-reflection, helping us see that humility about our limits is not weakness but the foundation for genuine expansion.

Why this lens?

Type Two's mechanism revolves around extending themselves into others' lives. They move beyond their boundaries, offering, fixing, loving, intruding—often without invitation.

Circle of Competence is chosen here because it calls the Two back to clarity: What is truly mine to give, and what lies beyond my capacity?

Reframing complements this by showing that "helping" can be re-seen not as a gift of self, but as a veiled plea for worth.

The GROW Model gives Two a practical way to explore this mechanism: clarifying their Goal, Reality, Options, and Will, rather than orbiting another's needs.

Exploration: The Two feels alive when needed, yet exhausted when unseen. Their "competence" becomes diffuse, spilling into others' lives. The trap is simple: equating being loved with being useful.

Exercise:

- **Goal:** Write down what you most want in a current relationship. Be honest: is it to be loved, to be recognized, to be needed?
- **Reality:** Describe what is actually happening in that relationship. Notice the gap between what you long for and what is.
- **Options:** Reframe the situation. Instead of asking, "How can I help more?" ask, "What if I did less? What if I simply received?" Write three possible actions that involve pulling back rather than leaning in.
- **Will:** Commit to one small action this week where you remain within your circle of competence—where you let someone else hold their reality without stepping in.

The Two's mechanism is not broken—it is brilliant. But when reframed through these lenses, helping no longer masks longing. It becomes a choice rooted in clarity.

The Mirror Self

Opening Lens

Probabilistic Thinking + Second-Order Thinking, through the GROW Model, opens awareness to complexity and consequence.

Probabilistic Thinking loosens attachment to emotional certainty, revealing that love and acceptance are never guaranteed—they unfold through countless variables beyond control.

Second-Order Thinking extends this awareness, teaching us to see not only the immediate effects of our actions but their deeper ripple effects across time and relationship.

The GROW Model (Goal, Reality, Options, Way Forward) structures this process: define a goal, face the real conditions influencing it, explore options by seeing their second-order consequences, and choose a way forward that reflects awareness rather than impulse.

Together, this lens cultivates humility and foresight—helping the Two pause before giving, to see what their giving sets in motion.

Why this lens?

The Two's mirror reflects a world organized around emotional exchange: *If I give enough, I will be loved in return.* But life rarely obeys such simple arithmetic.

Probabilistic Thinking reveals that generosity does not guarantee belonging—sometimes it even repels it. Love, like all living systems, follows no fixed pattern.

Second-Order Thinking deepens this realization by tracing the unseen effects of help offered too quickly or affection given as currency. When the Two's giving is driven by anxiety rather than openness, it creates subtle dependency loops—others feel managed rather than met.

The GROW framework turns this recognition into practice, helping the Two move from reflexive helping toward conscious, unconditioned presence.

Exploration: Twos often live inside invisible equations: *I give, therefore you should love me.* But every transaction has an echo. The more the EnneaType Two gives to secure affection, the more distance forms between giver and receiver. What feels like connection becomes quiet control. Second-Order Thinking asks: What is the long-term impact of this pattern? What happens to intimacy when love becomes strategy?

Exercise

- **Goal:** Write down the sentence: *I want to be loved.* Then ask probabilistically: What are the odds of giving more guarantees of love? What are the odds that it exhausts it? Let the numbers speak for themselves.
- **Reality:** Recall a situation in which you helped, comforted, or advised someone without being asked. Did it deepen connection or create subtle resentment? Write only what occurred—no explanations, no defenses.
- **Options:** Apply Second-Order Thinking. Ask: *If I act on this impulse again, what might happen next week? Next year?* Then, consider a new option: doing nothing. What happens if love is allowed to find its own rhythm?
- **Way Forward:** Choose one small experiment in restraint. The next time you sense another's need, pause. Wait until help is genuinely requested—or until silence itself reveals what is true. Notice how this alters the quality of connection.

This mirror exercise reveals how the Two's gift becomes pure when freed from expectation. When helping no longer hides a hope, love loses its price tag. In the quiet space beyond probability and consequence, love returns to its natural state—unpredictable, unearned, and utterly real.

The Path Beyond Type

Opening Lens

Rational Optimism + Cross-Pollination, through the GROW Model, cultivates a forward-looking stance that is both realistic and expansive.

Rational Optimism resists denial or blind hope, grounding positivity in evidence and possibility.

Cross-Pollination broadens perspective by drawing insights from diverse sources and disciplines, sparking connections that would otherwise remain hidden.

The **GROW Model (Goal, Reality, Options, Way Forward)** shapes this into a process: set a goal rooted in optimism, face the reality of current limits, generate options through cross-pollination, and choose a way forward that blends realism with creativity.

Together, this lens nurtures a disciplined confidence that is open to surprise, enabling reflection to move beyond habitual constraints into fresh pathways.

Why this lens?

The path forward for Two is not to abandon love but to see it through a wider field.

Rational Optimism grounds their longing—it is not naïve, but rooted in the reality that genuine connection is possible without manipulation.

Cross-Pollination opens the lens further, showing that love can flow in unexpected directions: from solitude, from nature, from Being—not only from people they serve.

The GROW Model structures this exploration into a forward movement: choosing a goal beyond compulsive giving.

Exploration: When Twos stop tying love to transaction, they discover love arising everywhere. Optimism here is not fantasy—it is a rational acknowledgment that love is the ground of Being. Cross-pollination shows that it can be encountered outside the narrow economy of "I give, you return."

Exercise:

- **Goal:** Write down one way you would like to experience love this month that does not involve helping anyone.
- **Reality:** List three current sources of love you often overlook (sunlight, silence, the presence of a friend, the warmth of a pet, your own breath).
- **Options:** Imagine cross-pollination: how could these sources mix with human love? For example, *can the quiet of nature teach me to receive affection from a partner without earning it?*
- **Will:** Commit to one practice of rational optimism: each day for a week, pause and name one instance of love arriving without effort

The path beyond type is not lovelessness—it is recognition that love has always been here, waiting to be received.

Closing Invitation for Type Two

Type Two has been given four lenses:

- Circle of Competence + Reframing
- Probabilistic Thinking + Second-Order Thinking
- Rational Optimism + Cross-Pollination
- All grounded in the GROW Model (Goal, Reality, Options, Will)

See what happens when you explore yourself through these lenses. Notice how each exercise pulls you out of the rut of compulsive giving and opens new skills for self-reflection. The invitation is not to abandon love but to expand your capacity to see it, to receive it, and to rest in it without condition.

Type Three

The Performer and the Loss of Value

The Human Mechanism

Opening Lens

Compounding + Game Theory, through Structured Problem-Solving, highlights how small, repeated choices accumulate over time and how those choices play out within larger systems of interaction.

Compounding shows that even subtle patterns of thought or behavior, when repeated, create powerful long-term effects.

Game Theory introduces the recognition that these patterns unfold within relationships, where each move shapes and is shaped by others.

Structured Problem-Solving organizes this into a disciplined process: define the issue, break it down, analyze possible strategies, evaluate their ripple effects, and select a path forward.

Together, this lens invites us to see personality not as isolated traits but as iterative choices interacting in a field of mutual influence, where transformation emerges from both inner shifts and relational dynamics.

Why this lens?

Type Three lives by accumulation: achievements, image, recognition.

Compounding reveals how small choices of image-building grow exponentially into a life defined by performance.

Game Theory reveals the relational trap: life becomes a competitive game in which winning and recognition define worth.

Paired with Structured Problem-Solving, these lenses help Type Three analyze not just how to succeed, but also how their success strategy itself has become the problem.

Exploration: The EnneaType Three is skilled at breaking problems into goals and tactics. But the hidden problem is the endless loop: succeed, be admired, and

28

succeed again. Compounding reveals how every small performance builds into a larger edifice of identity. Game Theory shows that in this game, others are not collaborators but audiences. The Three's mechanism thrives on visibility but starves the soul.

Exercise:

- Write down one recent achievement you're proud of.
- Trace its *compounding effect*. How many smaller performances built up to it? How much energy went into maintaining the image?
- Apply Game Theory: if this achievement were a move in a game, what "payoff" were you expecting? Approval, admiration, promotion, security?
- Using Structured Problem-Solving, reframe: *What if the real problem is not lack of achievement but lack of contact with my own being?* Write one alternative solution that involves resting rather than striving.

This turns achievement from reflex into inquiry.

The Mirror Self

Opening Lens

Agency Math + Design Thinking, through Structured Problem-Solving combines quantitative clarity with creative exploration.

Agency Math frames choice and responsibility in terms of variables and outcomes, asking what part of the equation is truly within one's power.

Design Thinking adds imagination and empathy, reframing problems through iterative experimentation rather than fixed solutions.

Structured Problem-Solving provides the container: define the challenge, break it down into elements, analyze constraints, prototype possible solutions, and refine through feedback.

Together, this lens highlights both the calculable and the imaginative dimensions of self-reflection, helping us see that freedom arises not from control alone but from engaging limits with creativity.

Why this lens?

The Three's mirror is polished, but deceptive. It reflects an image rather than essence.

Agency Math reminds the Three to measure who is actually acting: the authentic self or the performer-self.

Design Thinking disrupts perfectionism by reframing failure as iteration rather than collapse.

Paired with Structured Problem-Solving, these lenses show EnneaType Three that the polished mask is not the signal—it is the noise.

Exploration: The mirror convinces the Three that they are the image. But when they pause, they notice the exhaustion beneath the shine. Agency Math asks: "Who is making this choice? My survival self, or my essential self?" Design Thinking softens the stakes: every outcome is a prototype, not a verdict.

Exercise:

- Recall one situation where you performed or exaggerated success. Write it down.
- Ask with Agency Math: *Who was acting? What percent of that moment was authentic presence, and what percent was image?* Be honest.
- Apply Design Thinking: treat the event as a prototype. What would you redesign if you didn't need approval?
- Structured Problem-Solving: identify the *real* problem. Was it lack of value—or fear of being unseen?

This exercise reveals that the mirror of image conceals a simple longing: to be valued for being, not for doing.

The Path Beyond Type

Opening Lens

Leverage + Zoom In/Zoom Out, through Structured Problem-Solving, emphasizes perspective and impact.

Leverage teaches that small, well-placed actions can move much larger systems, while **Zoom In/Zoom Out** cultivates the ability to shift scale — examining fine detail without losing sight of the whole.

Structured Problem-Solving organizes these insights into steps: define the problem, break it down, analyze both micro and macro dynamics, identify leverage points, and act where the smallest shift creates the greatest change.

Together, this lens trains perception to recognize where attention and effort matter most, showing that transformation often arises not from force but from precision and perspective.

Why this lens?

The Three's path is not to abandon energy but to leverage it.

Leverage shows that small shifts in focus can create disproportionate transformation.

Zoom In/Zoom Out trains the Three to alternate perspectives: the granular detail of the moment and the wide-angle of life's meaning.

Structured Problem-Solving provides the scaffolding for applying these shifts to their deepest fixation: confusing performance with value.

Exploration: EnneaType Three already knows how to hustle. What they lack is the pause that multiplies impact. Leverage shows that stepping back may accomplish more than pushing forward. Zoom In/Zoom Out teaches them to see both the moment of performance and the lifetime of longing it reflects.

Exercise:

- Write down one current project you're striving to perfect.
- Apply Leverage: *What is the smallest shift in my approach that would release the most pressure?*
- Zoom In: describe the details of your striving—what do you do, say, feel?
- Zoom Out: step back. How does this striving fit into your whole life story? Does it mirror a childhood strategy of being valued only for performance?
- Structured Problem-Solving: redefine the goal. Instead of success, what if the goal were transparency? What would success look like if nothing needed to be proven?

This path shifts the Three from endless doing to radiant being.

Closing Invitation for Type Three

Type Three has been given four lenses:

- Compounding + Game Theory
- Agency Math + Design Thinking
- Leverage + Zoom In/Zoom Out

- All grounded in Structured Problem-Solving

See what happens when you explore yourself through these lenses. Each one interrupts the trance of performance, turning your brilliance for solving problems back onto the deeper question: *What if nothing needs to be achieved for me to be valuable?*

Type Four

The Romantic and the Longing for Depth

The Human Mechanism

Opening Lens

Second-Order Effects + Abstract Thinking, through Creative Problem Solving expands awareness beyond the immediate and the obvious.

Second-Order Effects highlight how actions ripple outward over time, creating unintended consequences that are often more significant than the original choice.

Abstract Thinking loosens attachment to the concrete, inviting us to see patterns, principles, and hidden structures.

Creative Problem Solving frames this process: clarify the challenge, generate possibilities, combine perspectives, test ideas, and refine through insight.

Together, this lens trains us to think beyond the short term and beyond appearances, revealing how personality habits sustain themselves and how new possibilities can emerge from a broader field of vision.

Why this lens?

Type Four tends to magnify feelings and assume their immediate intensity is the truth of the self.

Second-Order Effects asks the Four to look beyond the first wave of emotion to its ripple consequences—how indulging envy or dramatization alters relationships and inner stability over time.

Abstract Thinking pulls the Four beyond personal narrative into the larger patterns of being, where feelings are not private possessions but universal currents.

Paired with Creative Problem Solving (CPS), these lenses encourage the Four to shift from fixation on feeling to curiosity about possibility.

Exploration: The Four's mechanism treats every mood as revelation. But unchecked, this collapses into self-absorption.

- Second-Order Effects show how one indulgence compounds: a sigh of envy becomes a story of inadequacy, which becomes estrangement.
- Abstract Thinking loosens the grip: what if "my sorrow" is simply one iteration of humanity's sorrow?
- CPS offers a pathway from fixation to creation: feelings as raw material for something new.

Exercise:

- Recall a recent mood that pulled you under.
- Trace its second-order effects: how did it shape your day, your relationships, your self-image?
- Abstract it: write the same mood as if it belonged to humanity itself. What happens when "my grief" becomes "the grief"?
- Apply CPS: brainstorm three creative ways this feeling could be expressed (poetry, music, conversation, silence) rather than dramatized.

The human mechanism shifts: feelings are no longer traps but seeds of transformation.

The Mirror Self

Opening Lens

Formula for Happiness + Analogical Thinking, through Creative Problem Solving brings structure and imagination together in exploring fulfillment.

The **Formula for Happiness** reduces a complex pursuit to its core variables — conditions and perceptions that combine to create well-being.

Analogical Thinking extends this by drawing comparisons across domains, using metaphors and parallels to reveal hidden connections.

Creative Problem Solving provides the path: clarify the challenge, generate and compare options, apply analogies to test possibilities, and refine toward workable insights.

Together, this lens shows that happiness is neither random nor rigid, but an evolving equation that becomes clearer when we see patterns across different contexts.

The Four's mirror reflects absence: what is missing, what others have, what could be.

Formula for Happiness challenges this directly: happiness is not comparison, but the ratio of reality to expectation.

Analogical Thinking helps the Four see their longing in new metaphors: the missing piece as a doorway, envy as a compass.

CPS frames the mirror not as punishment but as creative material.

Exploration: The Four peers into the mirror and sees what is absent. But absence is not emptiness—it can be reframed as potential.

- Formula for Happiness reminds them: suffering comes less from what is, more from expectation.
- Analogical Thinking transforms distortion into symbol, reframing envy as a pointer to hidden value.

Exercise:

- Write down three comparisons you often make (to friends, colleagues, partners).
- Apply the Formula for Happiness: Reality – Expectation = Experience. Where is expectation distorting perception?
- Choose one comparison and create an analogy. For example, "Their success is not my lack, it is like a lighthouse—showing what is possible for me too."
- Use CPS: design one small experiment in which envy is treated not as proof of absence but as signal of direction.

This clears the mirror: longing becomes not self-pity but a guide toward wholeness.

The Path Beyond Type

Opening Lens

Double Think + Opposite Thinking, through Creative Problem Solving deliberately unsettles fixed assumptions.

Double Think explores the capacity to hold two seemingly contradictory ideas at once without collapsing them.

Opposite Thinking pushes further by asking what would happen if the reverse of an assumption were true.

Creative Problem Solving provides the scaffolding: define the challenge, reframe it through contradiction, generate options from both sides, test their viability, and integrate insights into a new understanding.

Together, this lens disrupts rigid personality patterns by showing that truth is rarely one-sided, and that holding opposites in tension can reveal possibilities unavailable to either pole alone.

Why this lens?

The Four's path beyond type lies in paradox.

Double Think allows two truths to coexist: "I feel incomplete, and I am whole."

Opposite Thinking encourages the Four to try on perspectives diametrically opposed to their fixation.

Paired with CPS, this breaks the trance of depth-as-drama and opens into depth-as-simplicity.

Exploration: Fours often believe they must choose: either dwell in pain or betray authenticity. But paradox dissolves this split.

- Double Think allows pain and joy to coexist, incompleteness and fullness to be simultaneous.
- Opposite Thinking breaks identification with longing by asking: "What if the very opposite of my story is also true?"

Exercise:

- Write a core self-statement such as "I am always missing something."
- Apply Opposite Thinking: write the exact reversal—"I am never missing anything."
- Hold both with Double Think. Allow both to be true for five minutes without resolving the contradiction.
- Use CPS: ask, "What new perspective could be created if both are true at once?" Journal or sketch whatever arises.

This path loosens the Four's grip on identity, opening them to the ordinary wholeness of Being.

Closing Invitation for Type Four

Type Four has been given four lenses:

- Second-Order Effects + Abstract Thinking
- Formula for Happiness + Analogical Thinking
- Double Think + Opposite Thinking
- All grounded in Creative Problem Solving (CPS)

See what happens when you explore yourself through these lenses. Each one disrupts the rut of dramatization and longing, expanding your skill for self-reflection. The invitation is not to abandon depth but to discover that the fullness you seek is already woven into every moment of experience.

Type Five

The Observer and the Retreat from Knowing

The Human Mechanism

Opening Lens

Occam's Razor + Systems Thinking, through the Fishbone Diagram balances simplicity with complexity.

Occam's Razor reminds us that the simplest explanation is often the most accurate, cutting through layers of assumption and noise.

Systems Thinking widens the lens, showing how parts interconnect and how outcomes emerge from their relationships.

The **Fishbone Diagram** integrates these two approaches: identify the problem, trace its contributing causes across categories, strip away what is unnecessary, and highlight the few essential drivers. Together, this lens reveals how personality patterns are both interconnected and overcomplicated, guiding reflection toward what truly matters without losing sight of the whole system.

The Fishbone Diagram in Words

The Fishbone Diagram, also called an Ishikawa diagram, is a way of mapping the causes of a problem. Imagine the skeleton of a fish: the "head" represents the problem you want to understand, while the "bones" branching out along the spine represent categories of possible causes. From each bone, smaller bones branch outward — specific contributing factors. By following the lines, you trace how multiple elements combine to create the issue. The value of the diagram is not in drawing it, but in thinking this way: breaking down complexity into visible relationships, seeing both the forest and the trees, and discovering which causes matter most.

Why this lens?

Type Five survives by retreating into thought, collecting knowledge as a fortress. Their danger is complexity—layer upon layer of concepts that obscure rather than reveal.

Occam's Razor interrupts this tendency: the simplest explanation is often closest to truth.

Systems Thinking balances the cut of the Razor, reminding the Five that simplicity does not mean isolation—every part belongs to a larger web.

Paired with the Fishbone Diagram, these lenses help the Five analyze their mechanism without losing themselves in endless analysis.

Exploration: The Five seeks mastery by gathering, hoarding, and holding back. Yet their mechanism complicates reality until it becomes unlivable.

- Occam's Razor slices through clutter: what if knowing requires less, not more?
- Systems Thinking restores connection: knowledge is not a private hoard but an interdependent field.
- The Fishbone Diagram offers structure: tracing each symptom of retreat back to its root cause.

Exercise:

- Identify one situation where you withdrew instead of engaging.
- Draw a Fishbone Diagram. Place "Withdrew" at the head. Along the bones, write possible causes: fear of depletion, lack of clarity, shame, need for mastery.
- Apply Occam's Razor: which cause is simplest and most fundamental? Circle it.
- Apply Systems Thinking: how does this withdrawal affect the whole system—your relationships, your work, your sense of vitality?

This shows the Five that withdrawal is not just escape; it ripples outward through the whole field

39

The Mirror Self

Opening Lens

Law of Cause and Effect + Chunking, through the Fishbone Diagram focuses on breaking complexity into visible, manageable relationships.

The **Law of Cause and Effect** insists that every outcome has contributing conditions, often hidden beneath the surface.

Chunking complements this by grouping details into meaningful units, reducing overwhelm and clarifying patterns.

The **Fishbone Diagram** provides the structure: place the problem at the head, map out major categories of causes as the bones, then chunk related details beneath them until the web of influences becomes clear.

Together, this lens trains perception to see not just scattered symptoms but how causes cluster and interlock, revealing both the simplicity and the intricacy of personality patterns.

Why this lens?

The Five's mirror reflects the illusion that withholding creates safety. But every withdrawal has consequences.

The Law of Cause and Effect shows that retreat produces the very isolation the Five fears.

Chunking helps the Five break down overwhelming patterns into manageable pieces, reducing paralysis.

Through the Fishbone Diagram, they trace the causal chain from withdrawal to loneliness.

Exploration: The mirror of the Five shows them safe in solitude, but the cause-and-effect reality is different: each retreat deepens separation. Chunking allows them to see not the entire labyrinth of life, but one small step forward.

Exercise:

- Recall one time you withheld your presence when someone reached for you.
- Use the Fishbone Diagram to chart the effects: what happened to the relationship, to your own sense of self, to your vitality?

- Break the pattern into chunks: What is the smallest step you could take toward presence without feeling overwhelmed? (One sentence spoken, one moment of eye contact, one shared breath.)
- Ask: *What effect would this single chunk have on the whole system if repeated over time?*

This reveals that presence grows not from mastery, but from small, repeated acts of connection.

The Path Beyond Type

Opening Lens

Locus of Control + Serendipitous Thinking, through the Fishbone Diagram blends responsibility with openness.

Locus of Control examines whether outcomes are attributed to inner choices or outside forces, shaping how we experience power and limitation.

Serendipitous Thinking loosens rigid expectations, allowing unexpected connections and discoveries to play a role in reflection.

The **Fishbone Diagram** provides structure for holding both: map a challenge at the head, trace the causes that fall under your control, and those that lie beyond it. Along each branch, remain alert to chance insights and unplanned influences.

Together, this lens highlights how self-reflection involves both agency and surrender — owning what is yours while letting the unexpected reframe the path.

Why this lens?

Type Five often believes life is outside their control, so they retreat into mental mastery.

Locus of Control challenges them to ask: What can I influence directly? What is beyond me?

Serendipitous Thinking expands their horizon, showing that not everything needs control—sometimes surprise itself is a gift.

Through the Fishbone Diagram, they trace not just causes of retreat but possibilities of return.

Exploration: Freedom for the Five comes from recognizing their circle of agency while opening to the unexpected. They do not need to know everything in advance. Life reveals itself when engaged with, not when solved beforehand.

Exercise:

- Draw a circle. Inside, list what you can control today (your attention, your breath, your presence). Outside, list what you cannot (others' opinions, outcomes, the future).
- Choose one thing inside the circle and commit to acting on it today.
- Invite serendipity. Ask: *What if life has gifts for me I cannot predict?* Write down three unexpected ways presence might bring nourishment.
- Using the Fishbone Diagram, sketch a path not from problem to cause, but from openness to possibility. What "bones" of engagement might branch out if you lived in curiosity instead of retreat?

This loosens the Five's grip on knowledge as defense and allows wisdom to emerge through contact.

Closing Invitation for Type Five

Type Five has been given four lenses:

- Occam's Razor + Systems Thinking
- Law of Cause and Effect + Chunking
- Locus of Control + Serendipitous Thinking
- All grounded in the Fishbone Diagram

See what happens when you explore yourself through these lenses. Notice how each exercise interrupts the rut of hoarding and withholding, expanding your self-reflection skills. The invitation is not to abandon knowing but to discover that wisdom arises most fully in participation with life.

Type Six

The Loyalist and the Loss of Faith

The Human Mechanism

Opening Lens

Regret Minimization Framework and *Nonlinear Thinking*, when paired through *Pre-Mortem Analysis*, cultivate a way of anticipating the future that learns from imagined mistakes before they happen—transforming uncertainty into foresight rather than fear.

Regret Minimization Framework, as a mental model, helps us orient choices by stepping outside the immediacy of fear or impulse and imagining how a decision will feel from the future's vantage point.

Nonlinear Thinking adds the capacity to see that outcomes are rarely straight lines; they ripple, loop, and branch into unexpected patterns.

Combined with **Pre-Mortem Analysis**—a structured exercise in imagining failure before it occurs—this trio allows us to expand the field of possibility while grounding it in reality. Rather than clinging to control, it asks us to acknowledge uncertainty, anticipate pitfalls, and still move boldly into open waters.

Why this lens?

Sixes live in a mind that prepares for collapse, a constant scanning for what might go wrong. Their loyalty is not blind devotion but a survival strategy—attaching to something solid in a world that feels uncertain. Yet this vigilance narrows their field of vision, replaying worst-case scenarios until all futures collapse into threat.

The Regret Minimization Framework reframes this orientation: instead of asking "what if it fails?" it asks, "when I look back, what will matter most?"

Nonlinear Thinking further disrupts the anxious loop, reminding the Six that outcomes are rarely linear and prediction is not certainty.

Pre-Mortem Analysis channels EnneaType Six's gift for anticipating danger into a structured, limited container—naming risks without drowning in them. What emerges is a shift from suspicion to foresight, from reactivity to grounded vision.

Exploration: The Six's engine is anticipation of failure. Pre-Mortem Analysis honors this, but moves it from compulsion into a conscious choice: if this fear were to come true, what caused it?

Nonlinear Thinking then bends the path, revealing futures that don't fit the old script of danger.

RMF anchors the process in long-term perspective: when you look back, which path—fear-driven or possibility-driven—would leave less regret?

This combination stretches Type Six from defensive rehearsal into creative foresight: from scanning for collapse to imagining a future of trust, abundance, and bold movement.

Exercise

- Write down a fear you've been circling.
- Run a Pre-Mortem: imagine the fear has already happened. List 3–5 reasons why.
- Shift into Nonlinear Thinking: now imagine three completely different outcomes, unexpected turns that break the straight line of collapse.
- Apply RMF: from the end of your life, looking back, which choice would you regret not making in the face of this fear?
- Compare. Which list shrinks you? Which opens space? Notice where the body tightens, and where it breathes.

The Mirror Self

Opening Lens

The Law of Motivational Beliefs and Devil's Advocacy, when paired through the Pre-Mortem framework, expose how unconscious desires shape perception by questioning success before it happens—turning anticipation into insight rather than avoidance.

The **Law of Motivational Beliefs** shows that what we believe is not passive—it energizes and directs behavior, often creating self-fulfilling loops. When beliefs are rooted in fear or doubt, they constrain action and reinforce anxiety.

Devil's Advocacy interrupts this by deliberately taking the opposing view, forcing hidden assumptions and unquestioned convictions into the open.

The **Pre-Mortem Framework,** which imagines that failure has already occurred and works backward to uncover causes, turns this into a structured practice.

Together, these approaches reveal how beliefs motivate action, expose their blind spots, and offer a way to consciously reshape the stories we live by.

Why this lens?

The Six's mirror reflects distorted beliefs: "If I prepare enough, I'll be safe." "If I trust, I'll be betrayed."

The Law of Motivational Beliefs exposes how such beliefs drive anxious behavior.

Devil's Advocacy turns Six's style of questioning back on itself, forcing it to argue against its fears instead of for them.

With Pre-Mortem as a grounding, this helps them separate reality from projection.

Exploration: The Six often confuses fear with fact. Their mirror shows them: "I am only safe if I am prepared." But when pressed with Devil's Advocacy, this belief begins to crack. They discover that safety is not proof against collapse, but rather the capacity to move with life, even when outcomes are uncertain.

Exercise:

- Write down one anxious belief (e.g., "If I don't double-check, disaster will happen").
- Apply Law of Motivational Beliefs: list three behaviors this belief produces.
- Become your own Devil's Advocate: write a one-paragraph argument for why this belief is false.
- Run a Pre-Mortem in reverse: imagine your belief collapsed—and nothing bad happened. What factors allowed safety despite uncertainty?

The Path Beyond Type

Opening Lens

Optimizing for Meaningful Metrics and *Heuristic Thinking*, when paired through the *Pre-Mortem Framework*, create a way of evaluating success that looks beyond outcomes to significance—transforming prediction into purpose rather than performance.

Optimizing for Meaningful Metrics reminds us that not all measurements matter—what we track shapes where we put attention, and many of the numbers we chase are distractions from deeper priorities.

Heuristic Thinking, the use of mental shortcuts, highlights how the mind reduces complexity into rules of thumb. While efficient, these shortcuts can also blind us to nuance and possibility.

The **Pre-Mortem Framework**, which imagines failure in advance and then works backward, forces a recalibration: what really matters, and what quick assumptions are steering us astray?

Together, these perspectives sharpen awareness of how we define success, caution against shallow measures, and encourage more grounded ways of anticipating risk and opportunity.

Why this lens?

Sixes often measure safety in impossible ways: did I anticipate every danger? Did I plan enough?

Optimizing for Meaningful Metrics asks: what actually matters? Not how many scenarios you ran, but how much presence you embodied.

Heuristic Thinking gives the Six simple, repeatable rules of thumb, cutting through endless analysis.

With Pre-Mortem grounding, these lenses shift them from vigilance into trust.

Exploration: The Six's deepest freedom comes from realizing they don't need perfect certainty—they need meaningful anchors. By redefining what counts as "success" (presence, faith, connection) and applying heuristics to stop spirals, they step into a more grounded rhythm. Fear loosens; faith grows.

Exercise:

- Identify one area where you over-prepare (work, health, relationships).
- Ask: What's a meaningful metric here? (e.g., "Was I present?" "Did I act with clarity?")
- Create one heuristic (rule of thumb) to stop spirals—for example: "If I've checked once, I won't check again."
- Run a positive Pre-Mortem: imagine a future where trust carried you through. Write three reasons why it worked.

Closing Invitation for Type Six

Type Six has been given four lenses:

- Regret Minimization Framework + Nonlinear Thinking
- Law of Motivational Beliefs + Devil's Advocacy
- Optimizing for Meaningful Metrics + Heuristic Thinking
- All grounded in Pre-Mortem Analysis as their recurring framework

These lenses stretch the Six's vigilance into vision, transform doubt into inquiry, and turn fear into faith. See what happens when you explore yourself through them. The invitation is not to eliminate danger, but to discover that safety is not proof—it is presence.

Type Seven

The Enthusiast and the Flight from Pain

The Human Mechanism

Opening Lens

Antifragility and Lateral Thinking, when paired through the SCAMPER framework, create a way of looking at problems that thrives on disruption rather than resisting it.

Antifragility is the principle that systems, like people, can gain strength and adaptability through stressors, volatility, and uncertainty, rather than breaking down.

Lateral Thinking invites us to step outside habitual patterns of reasoning, seeking unconventional or indirect solutions where linear logic would otherwise stall.

SCAMPER (Substitute, Combine, Adapt, Modify, Put to other uses, Eliminate, Reverse) provides a structured method for applying creativity in practice, systematically challenging assumptions and generating new possibilities.

Together, this triad reframes difficulty not as something to be endured, but as a source of innovation and resilience.

Why this lens?

Type Seven survives by escaping discomfort—leaping toward pleasure, options, and stimulation. But avoidance leaves them brittle.

Antifragility shows that engaging with challenge makes them stronger; joy deepens through contact with difficulty, not escape from it.

Lateral Thinking fits their playful mind but redirects it inward: using creativity not to flee pain, but to see new possibilities in it.

Paired with the *SCAMPER* Technique, these lenses give Type Seven practical ways to experiment with their own mechanisms.

Exploration: The Seven avoids limits, but antifragility reframes limits as opportunities for growth. Their creativity can be used not to spin escape routes but to transform discomfort into strength. SCAMPER becomes their laboratory: rather than avoiding pain, they play with it.

Exercise:

- Think of one discomfort you're currently fleeing (a boring task, a tense relationship, a lingering sadness).
- Apply SCAMPER:
  - **Substitute:** What if I swapped avoidance for one small act of presence?
  - **Combine:** How could I pair this discomfort with something I enjoy (e.g., music, movement, humor)?
  - **Adapt:** What small shift could make this pain workable?
  - **Modify:** Can I shrink it into a smaller, bearable step?
  - **Put to other use:** How could this discomfort teach me something about resilience?
  - **Eliminate:** What story am I telling about this pain that I could drop?
  - **Reverse:** What if I welcomed it instead of fleeing?
- Choose one experiment and try it for a day.

Pain becomes not an enemy but the doorway into aliveness.

The Mirror Self

Opening Lens

Forcing Functions and 10x Thinking, when applied through the SCAMPER framework, create a powerful blend of discipline and expansion.

Forcing Functions are intentional constraints that compel action by removing the option of delay, hesitation, or endless refinement—deadlines, commitments, or structural limits that drive progress.

10x Thinking, by contrast, is about radical expansion—aiming not for incremental improvement but for solutions ten times greater than what seems possible.

SCAMPER provides a systematic method to hold these together, guiding exploration through substitution, combination, adaptation, modification, new uses, elimination, and reversal.

This triad both pushes action forward and stretches imagination outward, ensuring that vision is not only bold but realized.

The Seven's mirror reflects distraction: noise disguised as freedom.

Forcing Functions interrupt this tendency by narrowing options, creating healthy constraints that reveal depth.

10x Thinking flips the script: instead of chasing more novelty, the Seven imagines radical transformation through depth.

Paired with SCAMPER, these lenses allow the Seven to test how focus and scale can liberate them more than scattering ever could.

Exploration: Sevens confuse breadth with freedom, but often their many options keep them stuck on the surface. Forcing Functions and 10x Thinking both redirect them: one limits, the other expands, but both push beyond the rut of shallow variety. The mirror clears when they see that true freedom is not running from pain, but living fully into presence.

Exercise:

- Identify one area where you're juggling options (projects, hobbies, plans).
- Apply a Forcing Function: cut your choices down to one. Commit to it for a set period (a day, a week).
- Apply 10x Thinking: ask, "If I went ten times deeper into this one choice, what could emerge?" Brainstorm wildly.
- Use SCAMPER to design an experiment that stretches depth instead of breadth (e.g., modifying one practice until it becomes a meditation).

The mirror no longer shows scattered distraction but the possibility of joy grounded in focus.

The Path Beyond Type

Opening Lens

Zero-Based Thinking and Pareto Thinking, when applied through the SCAMPER framework, create a rigorous yet imaginative toolset for questioning assumptions and focusing effort.

Zero-Based Thinking poses a simple yet radical question: If I were not already doing this, would I start? It clears the slate of sunk costs and inertia, forcing decisions to be made on current value rather than past commitment.

Pareto Thinking adds another layer of clarity by reminding us that a small fraction of causes often create the majority of effects—the famous 80/20 principle.

SCAMPER then takes these stripped-down insights and channels them into practical innovation, guiding attention through structured prompts of substitution, combination, adaptation, modification, new uses, elimination, and reversal.

Together, these approaches encourage bold resets, targeted effort, and creative renewal.

Why this lens?

EnneaType Sevens rarely stop to ask whether their choices truly matter—they're too busy adding more.

Zero-Based Thinking resets the board: "If I had to choose again, would I?"

Pareto Thinking sharpens the reset by focusing on the few actions that generate the most value.

Paired with SCAMPER, this combination helps the Seven step off the wheel of constant motion and discover freedom in essential simplicity.

Exploration: Zero-Based Thinking forces the Seven to confront their true priorities, while Pareto Thinking filters out the noise. Together, they reveal that freedom is not about having more choices, but about making meaningful choices.

Exercise:

- List three commitments or projects currently on your plate.
- Apply Zero-Based Thinking: if I had to start fresh today, would I choose this again? Circle yes or no.
- Apply Pareto: which one or two items create 80% of your energy, joy, or meaning? Which are filler?
- Use SCAMPER to redesign your week, emphasizing the essential and eliminating the trivial.

The path beyond type is not endless novelty but contentment—joy discovered in what is already here.

Closing Invitation for Type Seven

Type Seven has been given four lenses:

- Antifragility + Lateral Thinking

- Forcing Functions + 10x Thinking
- Zero-Based Thinking + Pareto Thinking
- All grounded in the SCAMPER Technique

See what happens when you explore yourself through these lenses. Each one disrupts the rut of gluttony and distraction, expanding your skill for self-reflection. The invitation is not to escape pain but to discover that joy is deepest when nothing needs to be added.

Type Eight

The Challenger and the Illusion of Control

The Human Mechanism

Opening Lens

Stress Testing and Confrontational Inquiry, when applied through the OODA Loop, form a powerful approach to challenging assumptions and surfacing hidden vulnerabilities.

Stress Testing deliberately exposes a system, plan, or belief to extreme scenarios to reveal where it might break under pressure.

Confrontational Inquiry goes a step further, not settling for polite questioning but directly pressing into blind spots and contradictions, often provoking discomfort to uncover deeper truths.

The **OODA Loop—Observe, Orient, Decide, Act**—grounds these approaches in a dynamic process: observing reality as it is, orienting through multiple perspectives, decisively testing responses, and taking rapid action in light of new insights.

Combined, they create a framework that not only identifies weaknesses but uses them as gateways to resilience, clarity, and transformation.

Why this lens?

EnneaType Eights trust force as their primary tool — act first, dominate, then deal with the fallout.

Stress Testing and Confrontational Inquiry channel that same instinct back into the Eight's own structure.

Paired with the OODA Loop (Observe, Orient, Decide, Act), the Eight's compulsion to react is slowed just enough to create reflection.

This lens is chosen because it forces them to test the necessity of control itself rather than only testing the world outside.

Exploration: Think of a moment when you were ready to impose your will on a situation. Instead of pushing forward, run it through the OODA Loop. Observe what is happening inside you, orient toward the fear of losing control, decide if the action is truly required, and act from clarity rather than compulsion.

Exercise:

- **Stress Test the Impulse** - Bring to mind a situation where you were ready to assert control. Ask:
    - *"If I did nothing for 10 seconds, what would actually break?"* List what is truly at risk versus what you assume is at risk.
- **Confrontational Inquiry** - Ask yourself directly:
    - *"What am I afraid will happen if I'm not in charge?"*
    - Then ask again: *"And beneath that fear, what am I really protecting?"*
    - Keep going until the answer touches something tender—loss, betrayal, or exposure.
- **Run It Through the OODA Loop**
    - **Observe:** What sensations, tensions, and impulses are present?
    - **Orient:** Notice the fear beneath the push to act. Let yourself feel it.
    - **Decide:** Is force truly needed here—or is it habit?
    - **Act:** Choose the smallest action that comes from clarity rather than compulsion.

The Mirror Self

Opening Lens

The Judo Principle + Dialectical Thinking, through the OODA Loop, opens the Eight to a deeper, more fluid relationship with power.

The **Judo Principle** transforms resistance into alignment—it teaches that strength is most effective when it yields, that energy can be redirected rather than opposed.

Dialectical Thinking complements this stance by holding tension between opposites: assertion and surrender, control and trust, self and other.

The **OODA Loop—Observe, Orient, Decide, Act**—grounds this awareness in continuous responsiveness. Observation invites presence before reaction. Orientation integrates multiple perspectives, including those that challenge the Eight's certainty. Decision becomes not domination but discernment, and action becomes attuned movement rather than impulsive force. Together, these tools train perception to flow rather than collide. They reveal that true power is not the will to impose but the capacity to respond consciously to life's momentum.

Why this lens?

The Eight's mirror reflects intensity. Life is experienced as a contest of wills: push or be pushed, dominate or be dominated. Strength feels like survival; vulnerability feels like threat. Yet the paradox is that their very effort to stay powerful perpetuates opposition. What the Eight calls protection is often contraction.

The Judo Principle exposes this illusion by showing that force met with force only multiplies tension. Yielding does not mean losing; it means aligning with the movement already occurring. Dialectical Thinking refines this further—each confrontation reveals a polarity waiting to be integrated. The OODA Loop transforms the Eight's natural decisiveness into awareness-in-action. It slows reaction just enough for wisdom to enter.

Power, seen through this lens, becomes conscious participation rather than control. The Eight learns that presence itself carries authority. When energy is no longer spent resisting, it becomes available for creation.

Exploration

The Eight's instinct is to act first, understand later. They trust their strength and intuition but often miss the deeper feedback hidden in resistance. Every push evokes a counter-push. The harder they assert, the more others withdraw or challenge.

The Judo Principle asks: What if the resistance you meet is not opposition but information? What if yielding for a moment reveals where the real leverage lies? In physical judo, the practitioner redirects the opponent's energy without aggression. Psychologically, this translates into responsiveness—allowing the energy of life, emotion, and relationship to move through without dominating it.

Dialectical Thinking deepens this inquiry by asking the Eight to hold two truths simultaneously: *I am strong* and *I do not need to be strong.* Both are real; neither is complete without the other.

Exercise

- **Observe:** Notice where you instinctively brace, argue, or take charge. Instead of pushing, pause. Sense the energy moving toward you. What does it reveal about your environment or your fear of being controlled?
- **Orient:** Reflect dialectically. Ask: *What is the truth in the other's position? What am I protecting by resisting it?* Let both stand without reconciling them.

55

- **Decide:** Choose an action that uses yielding as strength. Step aside, soften your tone, or invite collaboration. Feel the power in non-resistance.
- **Act:** Move deliberately and with presence. Notice how others respond when your energy becomes grounded rather than forceful. Let feedback guide the next loop.

This mirror exercise reveals that surrender and strength are not opposites but reflections of one another. The Eight's liberation lies not in more control, but in conscious contact with the flow of power itself. When force becomes fluid, will transforms into wisdom.

In that moment, the Eight discovers that real authority is not imposed—it radiates.

The Path Beyond Type

Opening Lens

Paradox Thinking and Negative Capability, when engaged through the OODA Loop, form a lens that embraces ambiguity rather than rushing to resolution.

Paradox Thinking invites us to hold apparently opposing truths at once— strength and vulnerability, certainty and doubt, control and surrender—without collapsing into either extreme.

Negative Capability, a term from poet John Keats, deepens this stance: it is the capacity to remain with uncertainty, mystery, and doubt without the restless demand for answers.

The **OODA Loop—Observe, Orient, Decide, Act**—anchors this capacity in an iterative process. Observation allows recognition of contradiction, orientation situates it within a wider context, decision accepts not-knowing as part of the movement forward, and action feeds back into a fresh cycle of discovery.

This combination trains the mind and heart to tolerate contradiction without collapse, to move with uncertainty rather than against it, and to discover that clarity often emerges not by resolving paradox, but by inhabiting it long enough for a deeper truth to reveal itself.

Why this lens?

Type Eights are action-driven; ambiguity feels intolerable.

Paradox Thinking and Negative Capability deliberately slow the rush to resolution.

The OODA Loop again provides a way of staying in contact with the unfolding: Observe the paradox, Orient to its tension, Decide to remain without collapsing it, and Act by allowing rather than conquering.

This lens is chosen because it trains the Eight to remain present in what cannot be controlled or forced.

Exploration: Notice a situation where your impulse is to act decisively. Instead of solving it, walk it through the OODA steps without seeking closure. Observe the urge, orient to the paradox, decide not to break through, and act by remaining present to what is happening.

Exercise:

> Sit with the koan: "What is your face before your parents were born?" Apply the OODA rhythm to your encounter with the question: observe it, orient to the mystery, decide to remain in it, and act by staying open. Notice what shifts when no resolution is sought.

Closing Invitation for Type Eight

Type Eight has been given three lenses, each carried through the OODA Loop:

- Stress Testing + Confrontational Inquiry
- Judo Principle + Dialectical Thinking
- Paradox Thinking + Negative Capability

Each one interrupts the illusion of control by slowing action into awareness. The invitation is not to lose strength but to discover its deeper form: presence that no longer requires defense, authority that does not depend on domination, and power that arises from being fully here.

Type Nine

The Peacemaker and the Illusion of Harmony

The Human Mechanism

Opening Lens

Choice Architecture and Polarity Thinking, when applied through Double-Loop Learning, create a disciplined yet liberating way of reflection.

Choice Architecture refers to the idea that the way choices are structured and presented shapes the decisions people make—subtle framing can guide behavior without eliminating freedom. It helps illuminate how defaults and passive patterns nudge action, especially for those who avoid taking a stand.

Polarity Thinking recognizes that many challenges are not problems to solve but tensions to manage: opposites such as autonomy and belonging, rest and effort, stability and change must both be honored.

Double-Loop Learning adds depth by moving beyond adjusting surface behaviors (single-loop) to questioning the underlying assumptions and beliefs that drive them.

Together, these three lenses show how to surface hidden choices, navigate opposites as creative tensions, and step outside ingrained assumptions that keep patterns repeating.

Why this lens?

Type Nine drifts into inertia by defaulting to others' preferences, mistaking the absence of conflict for peace.

Choice Architecture highlights how the way options are framed nudges behavior, allowing the Nine to see where they unconsciously yield choice.

Polarity Thinking adds depth by showing that harmony is not found in eliminating tension, but in learning to balance opposites—comfort and challenge, sameness and difference.

Double-Loop Learning provides the framework for going deeper: instead of just adjusting choices, Nines question the underlying assumption that avoiding choice keeps the peace. This lens allows them to reclaim agency without breaking harmony.

Exploration: Nines often equate stillness with safety, but this stillness can be a disguise for avoidance. Choice Architecture reveals that options are always present and can be shaped consciously. Polarity Thinking reframes conflict as a polarity to be managed rather than avoided. Double-Loop Learning then invites them to examine not just what they choose, but why they assume choosing threatens peace. Through this cycle, they begin to embody harmony as active presence rather than passive withdrawal.

Exercise:

- Recall a moment where you said "it doesn't matter" and deferred.
- Reconstruct the choice using Choice Architecture—list three clear options, including your true preference.
- Apply Polarity Thinking: identify the opposites at play (e.g., self vs. other, rest vs. effort) and ask how both can be honored.
- Use Double-Loop Learning to challenge the underlying belief: does avoiding the choice really maintain peace, or does it erode it?

The Mirror Self

Opening Lens

Contrast Effect and Pattern Recognition, when practiced through Double-Loop Learning, form a way of seeing that both clarifies and questions.

The **Contrast Effect** works by setting two elements side by side, allowing subtle distinctions to emerge that might otherwise stay invisible.

Pattern Recognition complements this by identifying repeated structures across time, showing how small behaviors accumulate into larger habits.

Double-Loop Learning provides the deeper framework: instead of merely adjusting actions (single-loop), it examines and challenges the underlying assumptions that create those patterns in the first place.

Together, these perspectives help reveal differences, recognize repetitions, and then ask why they exist—inviting not just behavioral change but a re-examination of the beliefs that sustain them.

The Nine's mirror often fogs because they minimize their own reflection, blending into the background of others.

The Contrast Effect makes subtle differences visible by placing them side by side—helping Nines see their voice in relief against conformity.

Pattern Recognition highlights the rhythms of avoidance, showing how small repetitions reinforce erasure.

Double-Loop Learning provides the framework to go deeper: rather than only adjusting behavior, it asks Nines to question the assumptions that drive their merging—the belief that speaking disrupts peace.

Exploration: The Nine often confuses quiet with harmony, but harmony requires distinct notes. The Contrast Effect reveals their unique tone, while Pattern Recognition exposes how often they mute it. Double-Loop Learning then challenges the hidden logic: why assume that asserting oneself fractures peace? By surfacing this assumption, Nines begin to see that real harmony emerges not from silence, but from inclusion of their authentic presence.

Exercise:

- Identify a recent decision where you blended into the group.
- Apply the Contrast Effect: write down what you said versus what you wanted to say. Place them side by side.
- Notice the pattern: how often do you repeat this? Use Pattern Recognition to name the triggers.
- Double-Loop Learning: ask what assumption underlies this repetition (e.g., "peace means not rocking the boat"). Question whether that belief is true.

Write down a new assumption that honors both peace and your voice.

The Path Beyond Type

Opening Lens

Option Value + Ecological Thinking, through Double-Loop Learning, brings together possibility, interdependence, and depth of inquiry.

60

Option Value (from decision theory and finance) highlights that even unchosen possibilities have value—having the option to act (or not) creates flexibility and freedom.

Ecological Thinking perceives reality as an interconnected web where each element affects the whole; meaning and impact are understood in context, through relationships and feedback.

Double-Loop Learning extends both by moving beyond surface changes (single-loop adjustments) to question the assumptions and beliefs that underlie our choices and our view of the system itself.

Together, these lenses reveal hidden optionality, locate each choice within a living field of relationships, and challenge the mental models that keep us stuck—so change feels less like disruption and more like participation.

Why this lens?

Nines cling to the familiar, mistaking stability for peace.

Option Value shifts perspective by showing that unchosen possibilities also carry worth—peace comes not from freezing options, but from holding them lightly.

Ecological Thinking loosens the grip of inertia by revealing that withdrawal unbalances the whole; your presence is a regulating force in every system you inhabit.

Double-Loop Learning strengthens these lenses by moving the inquiry deeper: it asks not just what choices are available, but why the Nine assumes that avoiding change maintains peace. The focus is no longer on surface-level adjustment, but on revising the belief system that equates peace with non-participation.

Exploration

For the Nine, the path beyond type is movement: the willingness to choose again and again, even in uncertainty. Option Value allows them to see every possibility as containing latent value—there is worth in keeping doors ajar. Ecological Thinking reframes "keeping the peace" as tending an ecosystem: absence has consequences, and presence restores balance. Double-Loop Learning then exposes the underlying assumption—"peace equals stability"—and replaces it with a more generative one: "peace includes my presence in motion." Peace emerges as a dynamic co-creation rather than passive withdrawal.

Exercise

- Identify one ongoing commitment that feels like autopilot.
- Apply Option Value. List three meaningful opportunities that would open if you changed course—even partially. Name the hidden cost of standing still (opportunities forgone, energy dulled, connections weakened).
- Apply Ecological Thinking. Map the small system around this commitment (you, key people, roles, rhythms). Where does your reduced participation create imbalance? Where would a small increase in presence restore flow?
- Use Double-Loop Learning. Write the belief that underpins your inertia (for example, "If I change, I'll cause conflict"). Ask: Is this belief true in this system? Who taught it to me? What new assumption would allow peace and presence to coexist (for example, "Peace deepens when I participate consciously")? Choose one micro-action this week that embodies the new assumption.

Closing Invitation for Type Nine

Type Nine has been given four lenses:

- Choice Architecture + Polarity Thinking
- Contrast Effect + Pattern Recognition
- Option Value + Ecological Thinking
- All grounded in Double-Loop Learning

See what happens when you explore yourself through these lenses. Each one interrupts the trance of inertia and merging, expanding your capacity for self-reflection. The invitation is not to vanish into others, but to discover that real peace includes your voice fully—peace as a rhythm you co-create with life.

The Path Beyond Personality

From Habit to Horizon

We began with a simple question: Why study personality? The answer has never been about fixing yourself or perfecting a type. Personality is a set of grooves carved into awareness—useful, adaptive, but limiting. The real invitation has always been to recognize the mechanism, see yourself in the mirror, and step into the path beyond.

Each chapter has offered a different set of lenses—mental models and systems of thinking—not to replace habits, but to disrupt them. To show that perception is plastic, that reflection can be exercised, and that awareness is infinitely more spacious than the ruts of type.

We explored each EnneaType through three lenses:

- **The Human Mechanism** (the psychological/structural lens)
- **The Mirror Self** (the perceptual/metacognitive lens)
- **The Path Beyond Type** (the transformative or practice lens)

Taken together, these lenses trace how each EnneaType functions, perceives, and transforms—the mechanism that binds, the mirror that reveals, and the path that frees.

- **Type One** explored *The Human Mechanism* through *First Principles Thinking* (seeking inherent order), *The Mirror Self* through *Critical Thinking* (seeing distortion without judgment), and *The Path Beyond Type* through the *DMAIC Framework* (refining perception into precision).
- **Type Two** examined *The Human Mechanism* through the *Circle of Competence* (knowing limits of giving), *The Mirror Self* through *Integrative Thinking* (holding love and autonomy as one), and *The Path Beyond Type* through the *GROW Framework* (transforming helping into presence).
- **Type Three** revealed *The Human Mechanism* through *Compounding* (efficiency as identity), *The Mirror Self* through *Metacognitive Thinking* (watching the performance of self), and *The Path Beyond Type* through *Structured Problem-Solving* (redirecting ambition toward authenticity).
- **Type Four** turned *The Human Mechanism* through *Double Think* (romanticizing absence), *The Mirror Self* through *Analogical Thinking* (seeing

63

meaning through contrast), and *The Path Beyond Type* through *Creative Problem Solving (CPS)* (transforming longing into creation).

- **Type Five** studied *The Human Mechanism* through the *Law of Cause and Effect* (retreating into analysis), *The Mirror Self* through *Systems Thinking* (observing connection within isolation), and *The Path Beyond Type* through the *Fishbone Diagram Framework* (mapping knowledge back to wonder).

- **Type Six** examined *The Human Mechanism* through the *Regret Minimization Framework* (anxiety as preemptive logic), *The Mirror Self* through *Nonlinear Thinking* (seeing uncertainty as intelligence), and *The Path Beyond Type* through *Pre-Mortem Analysis* (turning vigilance into foresight).

- **Type Seven** understood *The Human Mechanism* through *Antifragility* (thriving through volatility), *The Mirror Self* through *Lateral Thinking* (seeing freedom through constraint), and *The Path Beyond Type* through the *SCAMPER Framework* (transforming possibility into presence).

- **Type Eight** encountered *The Human Mechanism* through the *Judo Principle* (strength that yields), *The Mirror Self* through *Dialectical Thinking* (integration through tension), and *The Path Beyond Type* through the *OODA Loop* (awareness moving as action).

- **Type Nine** experienced *The Human Mechanism* through *Option Value* (seeing potential in stillness), *The Mirror Self* through *Ecological Thinking* (belonging through participation), and *The Path Beyond Type* through *Double-Loop Learning* (transforming inertia into harmony).

Each type was stretched by new ways of seeing. Together, they map a field of inquiry, not a set of answers. And personality was unmasked through Meta-Cognition and Systems Thinking, revealing not just what each type does, but what it conceals and what it still points toward.

What unites all of these explorations is this: personality is not a prison, but a prism. Light enters, bends, and refracts into patterns we recognize as "me." But beyond the prism is the light itself—clear, boundless, unpossessed.

Studying personality is not about polishing the prism;
it is about realizing the light.

For Coaches and Teachers

For enneagram teachers, guides, and coaches, these exercises offer more than a personal journey. They expand the repertoire of ways to meet students. Every client or student carries not just the habits of type but also habits of thinking. By introducing new models and frameworks, you help them step out of their accustomed mental grooves.

This approach multiplies your teaching tools:

- You are not only explaining a type but offering fresh lenses through which a student can see themselves.
- You are not just describing patterns but cultivating the skill of reflection.
- You are not presenting a fixed system but guiding an unfolding process of inquiry.

For the practitioner, this keeps the enneagram alive, dynamic, and creative—far beyond static descriptions of type.

For the student, it means freedom: the discovery that they can shift their way of seeing, and in doing so, loosen the grip of personality.

An Ongoing Experiment

You now have twenty-seven lenses and nine unique frameworks at your disposal. They are not tools to master but experiments to play with. Return to them again and again:

- When you feel stuck in type, apply a different lens.
- When you recognize your reflection, hold it up to another mirror.
- When you sense the path beyond, walk it with curiosity rather than certainty.

The Final Invitation

Ask yourself:

- What happens when I stop trying to improve my EnneaType and instead observe how it thinks and perceives?
- What happens when I see my personality not as an identity but as a pattern?
- What happens when I meet life as an experiment, not a performance?

The enneagram was never meant to box you in; it was meant to open you out. To study personality is to become intimate with the very habits that obscure freedom.

To explore personality through new lenses is to practice the art of self-reflection. And to walk the path beyond type is to discover that what you are is not defined by any number at all.

In the end, the work is simple: **See. Reflect. Step beyond.** Again and again, until even the need for steps dissolves, and only presence remains.

Epilogue

The Still Ground Beneath the Mind

The human brain is a magnificent instrument. It interprets perception, regulates the body, and ensures our survival in a world that never stops changing. It translates the raw immediacy of experience into meaning, weaving sensations into coherent patterns. It is designed to anticipate danger, solve problems, and organize chaos.

Yet this same brilliance creates confusion. The brain does not simply register perception—it reacts to it. Every sight, sound, and thought triggers a cascade of associations, memories, judgments, and imagined outcomes. These mental ripples arrive faster than we can notice them. The brain's interpretations, meant to protect us, become the very fog that separates us from direct contact with life.

What began as a survival mechanism becomes the default mode of experience. We live within interpretations rather than reality. The stream of thought captures attention so completely that we mistake it for reality.

We inhabit commentary rather than consciousness.

But the brain is not the problem; identification is.

We do not have to leave the ground of presence and lose ourselves in the machinery of thought. Awareness can remain at home, steady and grounded, while the mind performs its natural function. Thoughts can arise and pass like clouds across a vast sky that is never moved by their passing.

This is the shift that every contemplative path points toward: the realization that we are not the contents of the mind but the awareness in which those contents appear. The brain can interpret; perception can unfold while presence does not waver.

When this is apprehended—not conceptually but directly—something subtle changes in the rhythm of experience. The tension between being and thinking dissolves. The mind continues its work, but no longer in isolation. Its intelligence becomes transparent, fluid, and connected to the ground from which it draws power.

The movement of thought can then be observed rather than obeyed. Reaction becomes reflection. Reflection becomes seeing. Seeing becomes the still point of perception.

This book has been an exercise in that seeing. It has spoken to the mind in the language of the mind—not to feed its activity, but to open it. Every model, framework, and inquiry has been a way of tracing the mind's pathways back to the light of awareness.

The purpose was never to perfect the personality but to observe how personality forms, how it sustains itself, and how awareness becomes lost within its constructions. In doing so, the head center begins to remember its true function—not to dominate perception, but to clarify it.

Presence is not found by stopping the mind. It is found by standing still within it.

The thoughts continue, the body breathes, the heart feels, the brain interprets—but all of this unfolds within the stillness that is aware of itself. That stillness is not a product of the brain; it is the ground from which the brain, the body, and the world arise.

When awareness rests there, everything can move freely. Personality becomes transparent, thought becomes service, and life reveals itself as a single field of experience—unbroken, unowned, and endlessly alive.

Through your grace, the world will heal.

End of Book

A return to the beginning: the self that did not choose itself.

The Inner Architecture Trilogy

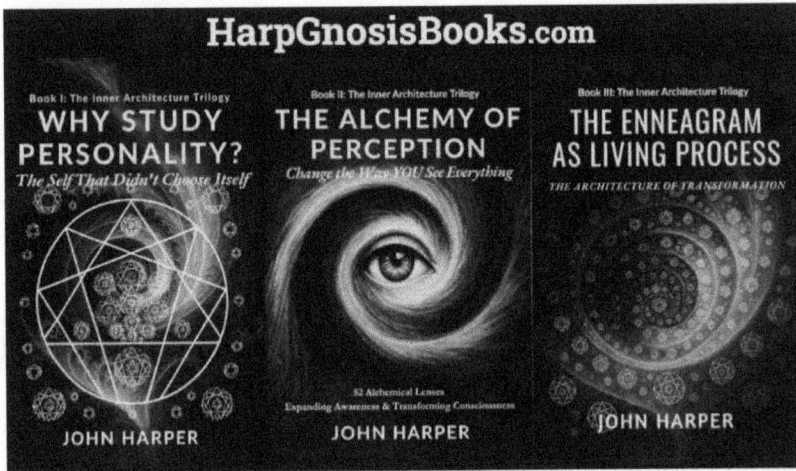

HarpGnosisBooks.com

Book I: The Inner Architecture Trilogy
WHY STUDY PERSONALITY?
The Self That Didn't Choose Itself
JOHN HARPER

Book II: The Inner Architecture Trilogy
THE ALCHEMY OF PERCEPTION
Change the Way YOU See Everything
52 Alchemical Lenses
Expanding Awareness & Transforming Consciousness
JOHN HARPER

Book III: The Inner Architecture Trilogy
THE ENNEAGRAM AS LIVING PROCESS
THE ARCHITECTURE OF TRANSFORMATION
JOHN HARPER

The three books in this trilogy form a single unfolding journey: from the machinery of personality, to the transformation of perception, to the living process that reveals who you truly are beneath the patterns. Each book stands alone, but together they create a seamless arc—how the self is formed, how it is seen, and how it is liberated.

Why Study Personality? opens the door. It reveals the architecture of identity, the three centers, and the hidden workings of the mechanisms that shape your inner world before you ever knew you had one.

The Alchemy of Perception deepens the descent. It shows how seeing is not passive but creative—how every moment is shaped by the way awareness meets experience. It refines the instrument of perception so the world can be encountered directly, without distortion.

The Enneagram as Living Process completes the arc. It presents the Enneagram not as a typology but as a living map of consciousness—how Being moves, how it forgets itself, and how it remembers. It shows how personality arises as an interruption in a much larger rhythm, and how the same rhythm contains the way home.

Together, these books offer a unified approach to awakening:

- a psychology with a soul
- a spirituality grounded in experience
- a map that brings all three centers—mind, heart, and body—back into a single field of knowing.

This trilogy is for anyone who senses that personal growth is not about becoming a better version of the pattern, but about rediscovering the one who has never been defined by it.

Understanding a child's inner world – and Yours!

EnneagramWorldOfTheChild.com

About the Author

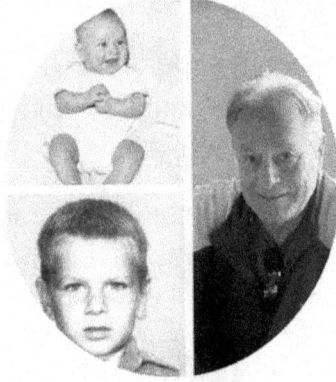

John Harper is a Diamond Approach® teacher, Enneagram guide, and student of human development whose work bridges psychology, spirituality, and deep experiential inquiry. His published books include *Nurturing Essence: A Compass for Essential Parenting,* which invites parents to discover the role essence plays in child development.

He is also the author of *The Enneagram World of the Child: Nurturing Resilience and Self-Compassion in Early Life* and *Good Vibrations: Primordial Sounds of Existence,* available on Amazon.

www.ingramcontent.com/pod-product-compliance
Lightning Source LLC
Chambersburg PA
CBHW081635040426
42449CB00014B/3316